Write Better Newsletters

Write Better Newsletters

Grow your 1:1 practice with emails people actually want to read

Camille Freeman

Copyright

Cover design by Lee Crutchley

Ebook ISBN: 979-8-9920338-0-9

Print ISBN: 979-8-9920338-1-6

From Fern & Ink Publishing | Staunton, VA

Contents

Introduction

In 2018, I left social media in the leadup to the midterm elections in the US, despite having a robust Facebook business page that felt very necessary at the time. What started as a month-long hiatus turned into a permanent break, and my mental health improved substantially. I worried at first that not being on social media would have a detrimental effect on my business. Instead, I've been able to grow my practice first as an herbalist/nutritionist and later as a mentor and educator for other practitioners using my newsletter as a cornerstone of my marketing – without paid advertising and without social media.

Over the years, I've mentored and supported hundreds of other practitioners and business owners in growing their own client-based businesses. I've found that newsletters are one of the best ways to bring in more 1:1 clients, particularly when you don't have the time or the stomach for heavy self-promotion or complex marketing strategies. When done well, newsletters can be fun (or at least not painful!) to write, and they can make a profound difference both to your readers and to your business.

Newsletters designed to bring in clients – whether your work is teaching private Pilates classes, seeing clients as an herbalist or a nutritionist, or helping people develop websites – are different than those designed to sell products or grow an audience. Most of us don't have the time to write long essays every week, and we aren't interested in growing a newsletter just for the sake of becoming known or gaining followers. Instead, we simply want to work with more clients. This book is designed to help you do just that.

I'll share a step-by-step process to help you design, write, and send a newsletter that feels like you and that your readers enjoy receiving. You won't be working from a stilted template that feels awkward, and you won't be spending hours trying to sound like someone you're not. Instead, I recommend a more personal approach that helps your readers feel connected to your work and provides you an opportunity to think deeply about how to best serve your clients and community.

Your newsletter doesn't have to be complicated, nor does it need to feel disingenuous. You don't need tactics and tricks. Instead, you'll focus on sending regular newsletters that reflect your work, that sound and feel like they're coming from you, and that your readers find helpful. If you do this, and if you periodically invite your readers to work with you, your practice will steadily grow over time.

This book contains everything you'll need to begin to grow your reach and write newsletters that matter to you, your business, and your readers. I hope you find it useful.

Chapter 1

Writing Newsletters That Bring in 1:1 Clients

When I teach a class or workshop on how to write email newsletters to bring in more 1:1 clients, I ask participants what's hard about writing a newsletter.

These are always the top answers:

- I don't want to send out junk that no one cares about.

- I don't know what to write about.

- I don't like feeling overly promotional.

These fears make sense. No one wants to write a newsletter that's generic, awkward, and/or pushy.

Here's the main reason so many newsletters are forgettable or unreadable: **The newsletter writer is approaching the newsletter as transactional rather than relational.**

If you think of your newsletter readers as a group of nameless, faceless people in a crowd ("they") and spend your time wondering how to get them to do something (read your newsletter, click on a link, become a client...), it's no wonder you don't enjoy writing.

If you think about your newsletter as a weekly flyer advertising your business or if you envision yourself as a puppeteer trying to pull strings to make readers take specific actions, that is indeed awkward and uncomfortable.

The types of newsletters that bring in more 1:1 clients don't require you to do either of these things. In fact, if you do them, your newsletter may not bring in many clients at all.

You may naturally be wondering how this method works, since your goal is to bring in more 1:1 clients. If you're not pushing people to sign up to work with you each time you contact them, how will you grow your business?

Heavy-handed or frequent selling does work in some situations. It's not always the wrong choice. However, when you're asking clients to invest their time, money, and trust in your 1:1 services, it's personal. Working closely with a client is different from buying a pair of shoes. People don't like to feel pushed into 1:1 work, and in fact, pushing often serves to drive potential clients away.

Particularly if the 1:1 work you offer is healing or requires emotional safety of any sort, people aren't (usually) going to buy from a stranger on the internet. They need to know you and feel confident in your work first. Also, they need to remember that you exist when they're ready to work with someone like you.

Rather than encouraging readers to buy immediately, we're building a relationship and offering potential clients the opportunity to get to know us before they decide to sign on the dotted line. Your newsletter doesn't need to include false bravado or weird marketing-speak. You don't need to be pushy or beg/strongly encourage people to sign up for your services.

Instead, you'll focus on sending useful or meaningful messages, which gives you a chance to share your own personality, perspective, and training with your readers. As you do this, your readers will get a feel for whether your work is a good fit for them.

In this book, rather than thinking of your newsletter as one-directional, meant only to serve you and your business, we'll set out with **the intention to create a newsletter that serves you and your business but also serves your readers and your community.**

To be effective, your newsletter will weave together your own interests, as well as those of your business and your readers.

- **You:** If your newsletter doesn't sound or feel like you, it's hard for potential clients to know you're a good fit. Without a sense of who you are, there's not much incentive for a reader to choose you over anyone else doing similar work.

- **Your readers:** If you write a newsletter that's full of professional details and personality but isn't helpful or valuable to your readers, they won't keep reading it. If it comes across as self-absorbed or isn't relevant, they also won't keep reading it.

- **Your business:** If your newsletter is full of helpful tidbits, your personality is shining through, but you hardly ever invite readers to work with you, share why they'd want to, or describe what's special about your work, people may not realize that you offer 1:1 services. You'll have great relationships with readers, but few clients are likely to sign up to work with you.

In this book, we'll go over **exactly how to craft a newsletter that addresses each of these while feeling fun – or at least not painful – to write. You'll learn how to write newsletters that matter to you, to your business, and to your readers.**

Handouts, resources, and links mentioned in this book can be found on the resources page: https://www.writebetterletters.com/resources.

We'll be working through the Newsletter Framework Worksheet from the resources page over the first several chapters of the book.

Before we begin, know that the most important things about your newsletter are that:

1. You send it regularly.

2. It feels like you.

3. It's useful or supportive for the reader.

If your gut tells you to do something that's not in this book or you've been doing something that's the opposite of what I recommend, please trust yourself. Nothing here is written in stone. This is meant to be a loose guide and a set of recommendations for those who like a bit of direction.

I can't wait to see what you create.

Newsletter Tip: Which newsletter provider should I use?

The major email service providers (ESP) on the market are all very similar (MailerLite, Kit/ConvertKit, Mailchimp, etc.). Most have free plans until you reach one or two thousand subscribers, which may take quite a while.

It's easy to switch from one to another if you have a relatively simple list. Therefore, pick one that feels accessible to you, start there, and know that you can change your mind later.

I use MailerLite for one newsletter and Buttondown for another and find that both meet my needs quite well. Mailerlite is intuitive and offers lots of bells and whistles for the money. I love the simplicity and support available at Buttondown. However, if you're already using a different ESP, such as

Flodesk or Mailchimp, and it's working well for you, then keep using it! There is absolutely no need to switch unless something about your current ESP isn't working.

If you're on an extreme budget and have more than one thousand subscribers, I'd recommend going with SendFox, which is basic but very affordable. For those interested in privacy and supporting a small business with great ethics, I'd recommend Buttondown.

The only services that I would not recommend *for our purposes* are Substack and its compatriots, which are designed for monetizing your newsletter. Substack is compelling because it's free to use, no matter how many subscribers you have (they do take a percentage if you start selling paid newsletters). However, it is very specifically designed for people who want to monetize the newsletter itself as opposed to the newsletter being part of marketing another service. This may not matter in the beginning or if you maintain a simple mailing list, but if you want to use Substack for anything related to marketing other than the most basic newsletter, you will run into substantial limitations.

If you find that you're spending hours or even days comparing ESPs and waffling about which one to go with, you are likely procrastinating on doing more difficult work. Pick one. They're essentially interchangeable.

The one thing you cannot do is skip the ESP altogether and send your newsletter through Gmail or similar using the BCC field. This is illegal. To comply with the law, people need a way to unsubscribe automatically, and you need to be able to prove that subscribers opted in and agreed to receive your newsletter. This is specifically what ESPs are designed to do. Don't reinvent the wheel, don't irritate people, and don't start an illegal newsletter.

Chapter 2

Newsletters Are Disposable

One of the hardest things about writing newsletters is the pressure we put on ourselves to create something truly remarkable.

Many of us start with the assumption that a newsletter needs to be professional, well-researched, and reflective of our skills and training. In our minds, it feels like what we're sharing will be written in stone. We agonize over every word and write/rewrite until it's perfect.

However, think about the conditions under which you typically read newsletters.

Most of us aren't sitting down on a Friday evening with a glass of wine or cocoa, curling up next to the fire with our beloveds to carefully read newsletters we've received, ready to jot down and savor the key insights from each one.

Realistically, people often scroll through newsletters in stolen pockets of time – while coffee's brewing, while waiting for a train, or when they're too tired to focus on other things – skimming the subject lines and maybe the first few lines of each message.

For most of us, it's quite rare to read every word of a newsletter, much less to save it for rereading later.

The way you consume most newsletters is probably how your readers will engage with yours. They'll skim through what you've written if the topic is of interest, and if they have time and if they don't get distracted, they may read the full newsletter. Most newsletters will be deleted. Individual readers will skip some or even most of your newsletters completely when life gets busy.

Newsletters are typically perceived by readers as disposable content.

As we dive into the nuts and bolts of creating a newsletter, may I gently suggest a small adjustment to your overall approach? **Don't think about newsletters as permanent and final work.** Yes, you want to put out content that matters. It's important to feel good about what you create and not to send junk into the ether.

Your newsletter will be received as something closer to a social media post – to be seen once (if at all) by most readers.

When we *write* newsletters, we think about them as foundational pieces of great importance. When we *read* them, we skim through loosely – if we get a chance to read them at all.

So far, we've covered two key things that may help you feel less pressure as you design or revise your approach to newsletters:

- You don't need to sell heavily in your newsletters.

- Readers experience newsletters as largely disposable pieces of content.

Now that the pressure's off, let's create a newsletter that fits your personality, your readers, and your business.

Newsletter Tip: Adding clients to your mailing list

Technically, in most places in the US, you can do add clients to your list automatically if you have a business relationship (i.e., they have purchased something from you). The question is, do you want to? I suspect you know how it feels to be added to a list that you didn't want to join. **A better**

option would be to ask the person if they'd like to subscribe when they become your client or make a purchase.

Some people choose to have a question about this on their intake form.

For example:

Would you like to join my [weekly/monthly/seasonal] newsletter for [describe who you write for] that [describe what they get]?

- *Yes, please!*

- *No/Not right now*

- *I'm already subscribed*

My colleague Liane Moccia came up with the "not right now" language, as she found that it feels more welcoming and doesn't ask your clients to reject your offer at the start of your relationship when they often haven't even met you for a 1:1 session yet.

Please note that if you have readers in the European Union (EU), you need to demonstrate explicit consent before adding someone to a mailing list. This means that you can show exactly where this person signed up and that they knew they were signing up. If you're using a freebie, they must also check an additional box indicating that they consent to receive promotional emails and/or your regular newsletter.

Also note that consumer protection laws change frequently. I am not a lawyer. To be super safe, **make sure that it's very clear that everyone who joins your mailing list intended to do so and recognizes that they're opting in to get your messages daily/weekly/monthly/etc.** See Appendix 3 for more information on the CAN-SPAM Act and other regulations.

Chapter 3

Your Newsletter Frequency

Designing your newsletter framework

Whether you're starting from scratch or revamping an existing newsletter, it's important to make conscious decisions about your newsletter structure, rather than jumping in without a clear direction. **When you have consistency in format, tone, content, and frequency of sending, your readers will know what to expect each time they receive one of your messages, which helps them come to know you as someone safe and predictable.** Making thoughtful decisions about your newsletter framework helps you craft a newsletter that suits you, your readers, and your business.

In this section, you'll design a framework for your newsletter so that when it's time to write your newsletter in the months ahead, you know exactly what to do. You're making decisions in advance – now! – to make life easier for your future self.

We'll go through each piece, step-by-step. Over the next six chapters, you'll:

- Decide how often to send your newsletter (here in Chapter 3)

- Identify your readers (Chapter 4)

- Develop a style guide for your newsletter (Chapter 5)

- Pick the type of content you'll include in your newsletter (Chapter 6)

- Create two newsletter templates (Chapters 7 and 8)

As we go through each step, please remember two things.

First, your newsletter is an expression of yourself. Think of this as an art project or an experiment with the goal not of following the rules precisely, but of creating something that you love based on a loose set of guidelines and advice. You can create something out of the box, or you can follow along with the framework provided in this book if that's more your style.

Although it can be scary to express yourself publicly in your newsletter, remember that people who sign up to receive your messages are genuinely interested in hearing from you. Your newsletter readers are typically one of the friendliest, most receptive groups you're likely to find in the online realm. Your voice matters to these readers, and they've signed up because they suspect you can help them.

Second, nothing in this book is set in stone. I'm sharing my best advice, based on many years of using a newsletter to successfully market my business and helping others do the same. However, your situation is unique. If you have good reasons for doing things differently than what I'm recommending here, please do them your way instead of my way. **You can break from my recommendations, and you can change your mind.** I suggest sticking with the decisions you make in these first six chapters for three to six months before making changes, as this gives you time to see what's working and what isn't. However, life doesn't always go to plan, and sometimes a fast pivot is needed.

If you'd like to use the Newsletter Framework Worksheet as you work through these chapters, you can download a copy on the book resources page: https://www.writebetterletters.com/resources.

Finding your newsletter frequency

We're starting with the easiest part of the framework. Your first decision is how often you'll send your newsletter. **In an ideal world, I recommend that most people trying to build a 1:1 practice send a newsletter once per week, on a consistent day of the week.**

However, a weekly newsletter isn't realistic for many new practitioners. You may have another job, caregiving responsibilities, or other commitments that mean you're unlikely to maintain a weekly rhythm.

If a weekly newsletter doesn't suit you, you can choose to send your newsletter every other week, monthly, seasonally/quarterly, or on another schedule (e.g., every new moon and full moon).

Sending regularly promotes visibility and name recognition

Sending your newsletter on a predictable schedule is a key part of writing an effective newsletter. Sending regularly means that your readers are being regularly reminded of you and your work.

Because readers are busy and often in states of information overload, if they come across your name once or twice, it's unlikely they'll remember you a few months later. **The more often readers hear from you, the easier it is to remember you when the time is right.**

If your messages are resonating, the right readers will look forward to receiving them. They'll have a positive association each time your messages pop up in their inbox. Even if they don't open the message, simply seeing your name and subject line in their inbox brings your work to mind for a brief second. (You'll learn more about the "right readers" in Chapter 4.)

Repetition helps people remember. If someone sees a message from you every single week about helping people balance their blood sugar, the next time cousin Fran asks about her hemoglobin A1C, a reader is more likely to remember your name and that this is something you help with. They can also search their inbox to find your contact info if needed.

Sending regularly demonstrates trustworthiness

Regular messages also demonstrate that you are a reliable person. They show that this work is important to you. You care about the readers, and you're prioritizing this relationship.

If your newsletter sign-up form says that upon subscribing readers will get a message from you every week but instead you send one occasionally or once a month, there's a lack of alignment. It's a small but real lack of follow-through. You are not delivering what you promised. We all make mistakes, but it's not a fantastic way to start off a relationship with someone you're hoping will trust you in a 1:1 situation. (If this happens, or if you're not sure you can deliver on a particular schedule, you may need to adjust how you've described your newsletter in your sign-up form. More on this in Chapter 15.)

Sending regularly offers more opportunities to practice and improve

Most people are not innately good at writing newsletters. Whether you're a proficient writer or someone who dreaded high school English (or both!), newsletter writing is a particular skill. Like all other skills, you'll need to practice quite a lot to improve.

When you send a weekly newsletter, you're getting plenty of practice. You'll develop your voice and style faster because you're writing more often. Your newsletter will become useful for the right readers over time, and it will get easier as you go.

Activity: Pick your newsletter frequency

Consider how often you'd like to send your newsletter. Pick a schedule that feels realistic given your current commitments. As noted above, I recommend weekly if this is feasible for you. If that doesn't feel possible, choose the option that feels like a gentle push without being overwhelming. Note your answer on the Newsletter Framework Worksheet.

Picking your newsletter frequency: a task list

- **Pick one of these frequencies**: Weekly, every other week, new moon and/or full moon, once monthly, once seasonally/quarterly

- **Select a specific day when you'll send your next six newsletters**. Add these dates to your calendar/schedule.

If you're planning to send weekly, which day of the week will you send? While there is data about optimal sending days and times, in my opinion it is not worth spending too much time worrying about now. If Sundays feel like a good day to send, plan on that. If Tuesdays work for you, that's fine, too.

If you're going with monthly, will you send on the first Tuesday? The twelfth of every month? Decide and add it to your calendar. I recommend picking a specific day of the week if possible. For example, you might send on the second Wednesday of each month or on the last Friday.

Similarly, if you're planning to send your newsletter seasonally, will you send it on the first Monday of each season? On equinox and solstice?

The day you send the newsletter will not necessarily be the day you write it. In fact, I recommend separating these two processes by at least a day.

(More on this in Chapters 11 and 12.) Therefore, don't worry too much about this now. Simply pick a send day and pencil it in.

Now that you have your next six newsletter send dates written down, give yourself a moment to honor that this is a real thing that's happening soon! Your first (or next) newsletter is scheduled, even if you don't know what will be in it yet. Congratulations.

Newsletter frequency FAQs

What if I want to send more frequently than once per week?

Some folks recommend sending your newsletter more often than once per week – twice a week, three times a week, or even daily.

If you have a specific reason to write more frequently, and if that fits into your schedule, then please go for it. Do remember, though, that it is possible to overwhelm people with too many emails. You're looking for a happy medium.

I recommend about once per week as a good goal to aim for when you're just getting started. I find that it's a challenge to write from-the-heart newsletters more often – although I have seen it done. Since your newsletter cannot be the only marketing/promotion you do, you need to make sure that you're spending your time wisely. (More on where your newsletter fits into your overall marketing plan in Chapter 15.)

I'm more of a spontaneous person. Can I send newsletters popcorn-style?

Is it okay to send newsletters popcorn-style whenever you feel the urge to write/send? Sure. If that's all you can do, then do it. You're welcome to send newsletters when the mood strikes.

Some practitioners write once every few months, some write regularly for a few weeks, drop off the radar for a while, and come back when they're able.

Remember, though, that showing up regularly is one of the main reasons newsletters work – particularly for folks who are avoiding or cutting back on social media. Seeing your name regularly helps people remember who you are and provides a sense of consistency that can build trust and confidence.

Sending newsletters only when you have something to promote is fine, but it does lean toward a transactional approach and away from community building.

Lastly, if you send infrequently, subscribers are more likely to forget who you are and mark your message as spam, which in turn makes it more likely that your messages to other readers will also wind up in spam/other/promotional folders. (The algorithms do not like it when people mark your messages as spam.)

What if I fall off track?

If you set a schedule that sounds realistic initially but then find that you cannot keep up with it, you'll be tempted to stop writing altogether.

At a certain point, you've fallen so far behind that it just doesn't make sense to try to catch up.

It's common to send weekly for a few months, until something comes up that necessitates skipping a week. After that first skipped week, it's easy to skip the next few weeks as well, until you look up one day and find that it's been months or even years since you've communicated with your readers.

If this happens, remember that **you are spending more time thinking about this than your readers. They signed up because they want to hear from you, and they'd rather hear from you less often than not at all.**

If your original schedule isn't working out, lower the bar until it feels more realistic.

If you'd planned on weekly newsletters and that isn't happening, try setting your schedule to every other week. Monthly or even seasonally is fine if that's what works for you in this phase of your life. You can build back up to your original schedule as your schedule shifts and as writing gets easier for you (it will!).

What if I feel discouraged or paralyzed?

This is the most common stumbling block. Particularly in the beginning, it can be challenging to build momentum. You may not have a lot of trust in yourself, and it's easy to compare yourself to other people. Writing to a list of five people can feel unsatisfying.

If this happens to you, remember that your newsletter is a service – a "give" rather than an "ask." You can help people with your newsletter, even in a very small way.

Also, remember that your voice is important. Showing up regularly is a way to show yourself and your readers that you're right here, ready to help. The specific way you say things is important, and just by writing, you can clarify your own approach to the work you do. Even if only five people read it, you have a chance to help those five people. Plus, the act of writing is beneficial for you as well since it helps you develop your own thinking and understanding of your work.

What if other things feel more important?

You started with good intentions, but somehow along the way other things felt more urgent and you never got to your newsletter. In this case, you didn't give yourself a chance to feel discouraged or paralyzed because you never sat down to write (or edit, etc.).

First, ask yourself if you are avoiding your newsletter because you know it may be hard. Almost everyone runs into self-doubt and a bit of paralysis when doing this work. Are you scared to start because you don't want to do something you may not be good at?

If this is true, I cannot recommend an accountability group enough. Consider a mantra or an affirmation to reinforce that you are enough and that you cannot get better at this without practice. That progress is better than perfection. Whatever you need to help yourself see that it's okay to be a beginner and that sending something out, even if it's not perfect, is the best way to start.

What if I'm not great at scheduling?

In this case, examine how you keep track of your tasks. How can you get your newsletter into that system for the next three months? Is it taking longer to write each message than you thought? Maybe you need to schedule an hour rather than 30 minutes. Maybe it would work to start writing a day or a week earlier, so you have more space to think and marinate.

Would you do better with a deadline? If so, consider pairing up with someone else who's writing a newsletter and committing to sending this person a draft newsletter by a certain day each week or month. They can review yours and you can review theirs if you submit them on time. Sometimes knowing someone else is waiting on you can be enough to move something up your priority list.

What if I have unrealistic expectations?

You might have had high hopes when you originally set your goal, forgetting that you only have five to ten hours per week to work on your business and most of them are spent working directly with clients. If you set your goals for how often to send or what type of newsletters to send with rose-colored glasses on, you may be feeling discouraged that you simply cannot find the time to get them done.

The good news is that you can reset your expectations whenever you want.

If you had originally hoped to send weekly or every other week but that isn't happening, some people have the tendency to just give up altogether. Instead of doing that, turn the dial down a bit. Take things down a notch and do monthly newsletters instead. Or shorten the newsletter. Maybe you send out a quick quote and an affirming note each week instead of a full essay and three recommendations.

Maybe you can share a voice note or a quick YouTube video. If video – or audio – is easier for you, do that instead and send it out in your newsletter. Create a "top three things I loved this week" message and call it a day.

You can ramp back up later. For now, if you haven't found the time in the last month or two, you aren't likely to find it in the next month or two either. Lower your expectations.

What if I have a major life disruption?

Lastly, sometimes you haven't kept up with your newsletter because life happened. Something unexpected came up and everything fell into chaos. Your kids got sick consecutively, your partner has a new diagnosis, your childcare provider fell through, you're moving, etc.

During these times, which are often unexpected and unplanned for, you may need to let the newsletter go.

If you're just getting started, perhaps it makes sense to delay the launch of your newsletter or to put the whole thing on hold for a while.

If you've been writing for a while, you'll have better data on how critical your newsletter is for the health of your business. If you consistently find that many or most of your clients are coming from your newsletter, you may need to prioritize getting it sent over other things – consider taking the frequency down, scheduling a series of "reruns," or shortening the format just for a while until things are more stable.

If you haven't found that the newsletter is particularly helpful in getting clients but are involved in a reinvigoration of your newsletter to try to change that, maybe you put it off for now and focus on the things that have been working.

Takeaways and next steps

- Sending newsletters regularly means people can remember you when it's time to book or refer.

- "Regular" can be weekly, biweekly, monthly, or seasonally.

- Pick a frequency, put it in your calendar, and send on those dates.

- If this frequency is not possible after one to two months, lower the bar. Send less often, but still regularly.

- If you can't keep up, jump back in when you're able.

Newsletter Tip: How do I get back into a regular sending pattern after an extended break?

If you fall off track a bit and ghost your list, all you need to do to start things back up is send a newsletter. It is truly that simple. You do not need a complex "warm-up" strategy. You *can* explain your absence, but you don't *need* to.

People may unsubscribe if they don't remember who you are or why they signed up in the first place, and that's okay. (More on unsubscribers in Chapter 5.)

Most readers won't notice at all. Remember that people are busy and that newsletters are disposable content for most people – it's a blip on the radar.

Jump right back in. You are probably overthinking this!

Chapter 4

Identify Your Readers

We're moving from the easiest step in the newsletter framework directly to the hardest step: identifying your readers. We need to be very clear on who your readers are before completing the rest of the framework. Please do not skip this chapter, even if you think you know who your readers are!

By "identify your readers," I don't mean that you should try to figure out who's currently subscribed to your newsletter and their shared characteristics. Instead, we'll be thinking about who you *want* to be reading your newsletter and how to write newsletters that matter to these folks.

Because this book is about how to build your 1:1 practice, it stands to reason that the people you want on your newsletter list are the people you'd like to work with in your business.

Writing to everyone is generic

If you write without a specific reader or type of reader in mind, or if you write for people who are not the people you want to work with, your newsletter will not be effective.

The number one issue that makes newsletters boring and ineffective is that they're generic. Remember that a newsletter needs to address you + the reader + your business. Your newsletter can't effectively serve your readers unless you know who those folks are.

Here's a scenario that may sound familiar.

Let's say you're a nutritionist specializing in prenatal care. You're writing one of your first newsletters. You've invited many people you know to subscribe, including family members, colleagues, former classmates, etc. As you're writing, you begin worrying about what your college roommate, who signed up for your newsletter and is a fancy investment banker, will think. What if you sound too woo-woo? They might think you're nuts. Or maybe your former physiology professor will think you sound like a simpleton who hardly understands a thing about this topic if you don't get into the weeds about folate metabolism.

Subconsciously, you start writing for real or hypothetical people who aren't potential clients. You're explaining neural tube defects from the beginning for your dad, you're showing off your advanced knowledge on zinc metabolism for your colleague, and you're highlighting your credentials and professionalism for your yoga teacher who hasn't even subscribed but theoretically might stumble upon your work eventually.

You get wrapped up in a vague idea of what sales copy is supposed to sound like and/or your email turns into a textbook chapter, with an introduction, background material, and 45 references. You're offering a masterclass on prenatal nutrition for people who know nothing about the topic and are unlikely to work with you anyway.

This is exactly what happens when you write for everyone. It's too hard. You don't sound like yourself, and your messages don't help anyone.

Instead of writing to please anyone who may possibly come across your newsletter, write for the exact people with whom you want to work. If the clients you're hoping to work with have been in the field for 15 years, you don't need to explain the basics even though some beginners may be on your list. Similarly, if your ideal clients are currently pregnant or trying to become pregnant, you can focus on topics of interest to these folks, without worrying about how to also provide benefit to people who are childfree by choice or post-menopausal.

Even if your mom is subscribed, even if colleagues are subscribed, do not write to or for them unless they are also folks who you'd like to work with professionally.

Write directly to potential clients

Don't worry about the therapist or doctor or copywriter or whomever else subscribed recently. **Write to be of service to the people you're hoping will fill your practice.**

The more specific you are about who you're hoping to serve, the more effective your newsletter (and all other types of marketing/promotion) will be.

If your clients are medical professionals, then write specifically to medical professionals, even if there are non-medical professionals on your list. If you're hoping to work with new parents, write exclusively for these folks, even if most of your current subscribers aren't new parents.

If you're uncertain about your niche or practice focus, pick a place to start, take your best shot at describing your clients, and move forward with this. **Understanding who you want to work with and who wants to work with you is a multi-year process because your interests will evolve with time and experience.** Your niche is formed largely by doing your work, which means that in the beginning, you will necessarily be working with mostly hypothetical information, also known as a guess. Instead of getting stuck here, point yourself in the right direction using any clues you have and begin working with real clients. You will gain more clarity with each interaction.

Take your best guess at who you'd like to write for and who you'd like to work with in your 1:1 practice. If you're not sure, here's an exercise that may help.

Activity: Identify your readers

If you're not sure yet who you'd like to work with and/or if you've got a vague idea without much clarity, you can use this exercise to point you in the right direction:

- Make a list of one to five of your favorite clients from the past year.

- For each person, note why this was one of your favorite clients. Usually this involves some combination of personal connection (you just resonate with one another!) and a great response to the work you did together.

- Is there anything these people have in common? What characteristics stand out to you about the folks with whom you most resonate? (Is it that most are kind? Busy? Welcoming? Parents?)

It's easier to write to people who like you

Once you've become clear on who your readers are, your newsletters will flow much more easily. When you're clear about who your newsletter is for, these types of people will be more likely to subscribe (more on this in Chapter 15). You won't be writing to a large, nameless audience of people who don't want to hear from you. You're writing to people who already like you and who are likely to benefit from the type of work you do.

These are the people you want to fill your practice with. You (presumably) don't want a practice full of clients like your mom or your colleagues. You don't want a practice full of people who doubt you or don't believe in the type of work you do or who don't love your sense of humor.

Instead, you write for people who are drawn to you and the type of work you do. You aren't bothering these people. They are predisposed to appreciate hearing from you.

Activity: Who are your readers?

It's time to fill in the second part of your newsletter framework. Note that this section will evolve over time. Take your best guess based on the exercise above and any other information available to work with as you complete the following prompt:

The people I want to work with/the people for whom I'm writing this newsletter are: [fill in the blank].

This is a key part of your framework. All other decisions are filtered through this lens. For example, we'll decide on a format for your newsletter next. Your statement on who you're writing for will help you determine what format would be most useful for these people.

Fill in the Reader Description section on your Newsletter Framework Worksheet: https://www.writebetterletters.com/resources.

Examples

Here is my own best attempt for my Practitioner Notes newsletter:

My newsletter readers are herbalists or nutritionists who are in solo clinical practice or who will be soon. They are excited and passionate about their work, want to provide exceptional care, and are sometimes overwhelmed by or reluctant to dive into the business aspects of running a clinical practice.

Does every single person on my newsletter list fit into this description? No. Definitely not. I have readers who are health coaches, acupuncturists, aestheticians, nutrition educators, herbal hobbyists, etc. These folks are welcome on my list, of course, but I don't write specifically for them. I filter everything that goes into my newsletter through the lens of the reader above. If it wouldn't be of interest or useful to that group of people, I don't include it.

Hints

- If your response includes any variation of "people who are ready to do the work" or "people who have the resources to change," you probably need to refine your answer. What does this mean specifically?

- At what point in a potential client's process would they most benefit from working with you? Would you rather work with someone who's just started trying to conceive or someone who has been trying for years without becoming pregnant? Does your web design work most benefit people who are creating their very first website or those who've been DIYing it forever and are now ready to level up?

- It's common for people to get stuck around niching. I recommend spending no more than 15 to 30 minutes filling in this part of the framework. Perfectionists, I'm speaking specifically to you. You will not have a perfect response to this part of the framework, particularly if you are in the first few years of your business. Make a guess, revisit it once you have more information, and move ahead.

- Mark Silver's book, *Heart-Centered Business,* has excellent advice on how to think about and describe the types of people with whom you want to work.

Takeaways and next steps

- If you write without a specific reader or type of reader in mind, or if you write for people who are not the people who you want to work with, your newsletter will not be effective.

- Write your newsletters for the people who you would most like to work with.

- Complete the "Reader Description" portion of the newsletter framework.

- Your description of readers will likely change over time; this is normal and expected as you continue to do your work.

Newsletter Tip: Writing to no one

It can feel awkward or difficult to write into the void when you're starting a newsletter. You may even be writing exclusively to imaginary future readers at first. It's common to feel unmoored, unsure, and even a little bit foolish writing your first message (and often your second, third, and fourth as well). In some ways, it can feel like journaling, but in public.

My suggestion is to remember three things if you find yourself writing to a teeny-tiny list:

- **Pretend you're writing an email specifically to a client you loved working with.** My brain and heart understand that this specific person I'm writing to may or may not read my message right away, but that eventually it will reach them. Visualize that person and write a message that they might find helpful.

- **The beauty of a teeny-tiny list is that hardly anyone will read what you write.** You get to be awkward. You get to change your tone and careen from one format to another as you find your style and rhythm. It's best to do this with a small audience!

- **There is no way to make this less awkward** other than posting your first newsletter. And then your second. And then your third. Truly, there isn't a shortcut or a hack to make this part easier.

Chapter 5

Select Your Newsletter Style

We've talked about who your readers are or will be. Now, let's think about how to create a newsletter that feels like you.

You want to send out something that reflects your ethos and what's special about the work you do. **Nuanced decisions like the way you address your readers, the type of content you send, and the tone you use when writing all add up to give readers a specific impression of you and your work.** It's hard for potential clients to find anything with which to resonate in a generic piece of writing.

To craft a newsletter that feels like you, you'll first need to have a good sense of your business or practice mission and values, how you show up in the world, and what would make a client choose you over someone who does similar work.

Activity: Describe your business values

Pick three to four adjectives that describe you and your vision for your work.

Think about the way you show up for your clients. What feel do you want to bring to interactions? What words have others used to describe you or your work?

If someone were choosing between you and a colleague who is equally qualified and does the same type of work you do, how might you help them choose? (Go to this person if you want XXX, come work with me if you want XXX.)

For example, the words I use to guide my business are *bright, clear, curious,* and *authentic*.

Here are some adjectives to consider. If you're stuck, you can ask former clients, colleagues, or others who are familiar with your work for help. While this list is a starting place, I encourage you to add your own descriptors, too.

- Warm

- Intuitive

- Practical

- Compassionate

- Reliable

- Curious

- Empowering

- Supportive

- Authentic

- Creative

- Passionate

- Collaborative

- Academic

- Approachable

- Meticulous

- Sarcastic/funny

- Analytical

- Brainy

- Thorough

- Calm

- Empathetic

- Quiet

- Enthusiastic

- Weird or wacky

- Simple

It's important not to **pick words that are aspirational, but rather ones that reflect who you are now and how you show up day in and day out in your work with clients.** Which ones are particular strengths? Which ones can people count on you for?

Another way to think about this: How do you want clients to feel when they're finished working with you?

Pick three or four adjectives that serve as guideposts for how you show up in your work. You'll want your newsletter to reflect these as well. Add these to your Newsletter Framework Worksheet.

How to address your readers

Now that you have a clear idea of who you're writing for and how you want to show up in your writing, you'll make a series of small, mostly one-time decisions that have a significant impact on the tone and feel for your newsletter, including:

- Which salutation you'll use

- Whether to use placeholders

- Whether to use the singular or plural when addressing readers

- Which sign-off you'll use

Your salutation or greeting

The very first thing a reader will see when opening your newsletter is the greeting or salutation you choose. **If you decide now how you want to greet your readers and note your choice on the Newsletter Framework Worksheet, you won't need to expend energy on deciding/remembering each time you write a newsletter.**

You can always skip a greeting altogether if that fits the tone you're going for.

Otherwise, you'll want to choose a greeting that aligns with the descriptive words you chose above. As you consider which greeting to use, there are two smaller decisions to make:

1. Will you use placeholders in your messages?

2. Will you address your readers in the singular or in the plural?

Deciding whether to use placeholders

You may have noticed that some newsletters you receive incorporate your name in the salutation and/or in the body of the email. This is accomplished by using placeholders when writing your newsletter.

In case you're not familiar with the term "placeholder," these are essentially small pieces of software sorcery that allow you to enter a tag or phrase that is replaced with individualized data to personalize your newsletter.

For example, you can write in your newsletter:

Dear {firstname},

And your ESP will replace {firstname} with each individual person's first name (or whatever they've entered in the "first name" field when they signed up). Note that the actual phrase/characters for doing this are different for each ESP.

You'll occasionally see these sprinkled into the body of a newsletter you receive:

"And so, Camille, I turned away from the frog and never went back to the pond."

Pros and cons of using placeholders

Placeholders serve to personalize newsletters. The intention is to increase engagement and to help the reader feel more interested in the message and/or more connected to your work. The data bears this out: We are more likely to keep reading when we see our own names, and various studies do show that readers are more likely to open, click, or buy when their name is used.

However, using someone's name in this way does have some downsides as well. It can be perceived as intrusive or insincere. Placeholders are meant to simulate a message sent from one person to another, when in fact, this is not a personalized message. There are also some technical challenges to consider. First, if you don't set this up correctly, you run the risk of sending out a message that shows up in the reader's inbox saying *"Hi [firstname]"* rather than their actual name. Yikes.

Also, placeholders rely on the data entered by your reader when they sign up. Sometimes people put odd things in the "first name" field or misspell their own name. If you don't keep up with the data and double-check, you may wind up sending out messages with the salutation, *"Dear DO NOT SELL MY INFORMATION"* or *"Hi, Btetsy."*

Singular or plural?

If you decide to use placeholders, you'll be addressing your readers in the singular. The rest of us will also need to decide whether to use singular nouns (*Dear one,*) or plural nouns (*Dear ones,*) when addressing readers.

If you use singular nouns, this can create a more personal feel to your newsletter. However, since you are not actually writing to a single person, using singular nouns may feel inauthentic or forced.

Plural nouns acknowledge that the message is going to many people rather than just one and may also help build a sense of community or belonging (particularly if you name your readers – e.g., *Hi, Herbies*, or *Happy Monday, Washingtonians.*). However, using plural nouns also comes with a more formal or distant tone, which may not reflect the tone you wish to convey.

Example

When I see that my name has clearly been added using a placeholder in an email I receive, it feels mildly disingenuous to me. So I don't use them in my own newsletters. I do, however, use singular nouns when writing. The tone I'm hoping to convey is casual, clear, and friendly. I want to envision helping individual people when I'm writing, without adding someone's actual name, which feels like crossing the line to me.

Your lines may be in different places. You might love the feel of using people's names in your messages, or you may have specific reasons to use plural nouns as you address your readers.

Go ahead and **decide now whether you want to use placeholders or not, and if not, whether you'd like to address your readers using singular or plural nouns.** Add your choices to your Newsletter Framework Worksheet.

Choose your greeting or salutation

Now that you've made choices about placeholders and singular versus plural nouns, let's get more specific about which salutation you'll use to open your newsletters.

My favorite is "Hi there."

Some other options (in most of these examples, you can insert a placeholder to add first names if you choose):

- Dear friend, or Dear [firstname],

- Hello again, or Hello again, [firstname],

- Hey, you. Or Hey, [firstname].

- Greetings. Or Greetings, [firstname].

- Greetings, Earthling.

You can also play around with these greetings, with or without placeholders added:

- Howdy

- Hey

- Ahoy

- Hello

- Hiya

- Salutations

You could start out by saying *"Good morning/afternoon/evening/day."* If you're multilingual, perhaps you could use a salutation that blends multiple languages.

When in doubt, pick a greeting you would use when writing an email or a letter. If you can see yourself saying or writing this greeting in another context, it's probably a reasonable choice. Also, pick a greeting that aligns with the words you chose to describe your practice. If you picked "academic," "meticulous," and "formal," then *"Hiya*!" most likely isn't your best bet for a greeting.

If you'd like to call your readers something without using their actual names, you could consider nouns like these: Herbies, changemaker, visionary, innovator, beloveds, friends.

Author and podcaster KC Davis calls listeners *"sentient balls of stardust."* Business mentor Leonie Dawson uses a constantly changing stream of terms like *"pookie bears," "peony," "dearests," "hi darling [name],"* *"blossoms," "darlinghearts,"* and *"patooties,"* to name a few.

Ann Handley, marketer and author of *Everybody Writes*, also uses a variety of salutations in her newsletter *Total Annarchy*. A short sampling of her latest options include *"Hello, Sunshine!" "Hey, hot stuff." "Hello, gorgeous!"* *"What's the word, baby bird?"* and *"Avast, m'hearties."*

Choosing your sign-off

Similarly, you'll want to have a regular sign-off at the end of your newsletter. Select one that aligns with the adjectives you chose to describe your practice above.

I use:

Take care, Camille

Mainly because that's how I end most emails that I write 1:1. It feels very me, for now.

Here are some other options to consider:

- Sincerely,

- Cheers,

- All my best (or All the best),

- Stay well,

- Until next time,

- Talk soon,

- Warmly,

- With love/care/a smile/etc.

- Or you can get fancy:

    - With _____ and _____,

    - Stay _____ and _____,

Examples

- Kristen Mastel uses "love and lemon balm,"

- Mark Silver, whose business motto is "every act of business can be an act of love," signs off with "With love, Mark"

Takeaways and next steps

Fill in Part 4 on your Newsletter Framework Worksheet. Remember, you're aiming for a newsletter that sounds and feels like you so that your clients can get a feel for who you are, what you value, and what it might be like to work with you.

- Select three to four adjectives that describe how you want to show up in your work.

- Use these adjectives to guide you as you craft your newsletter, in combination with your understanding of what may serve your readers.

- Decide whether to use placeholders.

- Decide whether to use singular or plural nouns to address your readers.

- Decide on a greeting.

- Decide on a sign-off.

Newsletter Tip: Unsubscribers

You know this, and I'm going to say it anyway: People will unsubscribe from your newsletter.

Especially in the beginning, you may get a sinking feeling in your stomach when you see your subscriber count go down rather than up.

It feels like a mini rejection during a vulnerable phase of your business. It doesn't feel great to see that number drop, but people unsubscribing is part of writing a newsletter.

Why people unsubscribe

Here are a few things to remember about unsubscribers:

1. People unsubscribe for a variety of reasons, and only some of them have to do with you and the content of your newsletter. Sometimes people unsubscribe because they're switching to a new email address. Sometimes they're on an unsubscribing rampage that involves removing themselves from all mailing lists. Sometimes they've moved on and are no longer interested in the type of thing you do. Sometimes the topic of your newsletter is painful to them, and they unsubscribe for that reason. For example, if your work centers around fertility and prenatal care, like mine does, people may unsubscribe if they've had a recent pregnancy loss or if they've decided to stop trying for a baby.

2. Sometimes a reader will unsubscribe because of you or the content you're writing. While it does sting, I typically interpret this as a good sign. If you're sending newsletters that take a stand, ones that show your work and your philosophy, you will likely drive some people away because the fit isn't right. They do not resonate with what you're doing, they don't want the kind of work you're offering, or they don't mesh well with your personality. **If you're showing up strongly enough for people to know that you're not the right fit, then it's also possible for other people to determine you ARE the right fit.** Remember: It's better to have a small group of people who are drawn to the way you do your work than it is to have a large group of readers who are vaguely interested in the topic but don't really care one way or the other about your perspective.

If someone doesn't resonate with the type of work you do, or even if they just find you irritating (some people will!), it doesn't necessarily mean you need to change. There's a lid for every pot, and while you won't be the right choice for everyone, you're the perfect fit for some, and those are the people for whom you're writing.

How to handle unsubscribers: mental health tips

Even if you fully understand the many and varied reasons that folks unsubscribe, and even if you theoretically understand that it's a good thing for folks who aren't in alignment with you/your work to leave your list, it's still a bummer when people unsubscribe.

Here's how to handle it:

1. Acknowledge that it's disappointing. Wallow a bit if you need to. This gets easier with time.

2. Remind yourself that you get to choose how to think about why they unsubscribed. You can choose to believe your newsletter is awful, or you can choose to believe that it wasn't a good fit for this person right now and that there are no hard feelings.

3. Bless and release this person. Spend your time and energy serving the people who do want to hear from you.

How to handle unsubscribers: logistical tips

If you're using an ESP, the system will automatically remove this person from your list when they click the "unsubscribe" button. There's nothing else you need to do on your end.

All ESPs should have the option to choose how/when/whether you are notified about new subscribers and unsubscribers. **Do not get immediate notifications when someone unsubscribes.** I recommend getting a daily or a weekly summary delivered via email.

For the record, I don't recommend investigating who unsubscribed and gently stalking them. Mentally wish them well, and then let it go.

You can set up a quick survey in most ESPs asking people why they unsubscribed. Most people won't fill it out, but a few will. Review the results of this survey once every three to four months or so.

Unsubcribers are normal when you send an email after taking an extended break. If someone doesn't remember who you are or why they signed up for the list because they haven't heard from you in a few months (years?!), you'll see more unsubscribers. You will also see more unsubscribers when you send out an offer or invitation email. Remember, if a periodic invitation to work with you is so upsetting that a reader doesn't want to hear from you anymore, they weren't a good fit anyway. You don't want a list full of people who are never going to work with you.

Chapter 6

Select Your Newsletter Sections

Newsletters come in all shapes and sizes. In this section, you'll choose which sections to include in your newsletter, keeping both your preferences and personality and your readers' interests in mind.

Your goal is to send newsletters that serve your readers and highlight your compassion, your skill, and your specific approach to the work you do. You don't necessarily need to write long, intensive, or heavily researched articles to do this.

In fact, most readers don't have time to or interest in reading long or complex essays in newsletter format on a regular basis. Remember that newsletters are mostly disposable content, read in stolen moments of time between other activities. **For the most part, your newsletter will be more helpful to your readers if it's short, to the point, and very specific to their interests/needs.**

The very name "newsletter" is misleading, since newsletters don't have to contain news and they don't have to be letters. There isn't a single correct or optimal way to structure them (although I will argue later that there are some wrong ways).

Your newsletter does not need to be an essay or a story (although it can be these things!).

It doesn't need to be long.

A newsletter can be straightforward and simple.

It can be a list of upcoming events in your community or a roundup of relevant links. It might be a single, easy recipe delivered every Tuesday.

Your newsletter might be a weekly word of encouragement or a video meditation that goes out on the full moon each month.

Using newsletters to alert readers that you've published a blog post, video, or podcast is also perfectly fine.

Hopefully, these ideas have your wheels turning. The next activity will give you additional ideas to contemplate for your own newsletter.

Activity: Which newsletters do you enjoy?

As you decide what type of newsletter you want to send, it can be helpful to review the types of newsletters you like to receive. There's a good chance that you and your clients are remarkably similar in some ways, including this one.

Take a moment to scroll through the email newsletters you've received over the last two to four weeks. Why did you originally subscribe to them? Which ones do you open consistently? Why? What do you notice about the tone, format, and value of the newsletters that you do read some or all the time? Take special note of the various sections included in your favorite newsletters.

See the book resources page for a download you can use to keep notes on the newsletters you receive, which may help inspire you as you create your own.

How your newsletter might serve readers

As you scroll through the newsletters you've received lately, you may notice that you appreciate each one for slightly different reasons. Newsletters can serve different roles; deciding which of these you'd like to offer your readers will help you craft the right type of newsletter for your business.

Here are some general types of newsletters:

1. **Promotional:** Intended to directly promote a service or product(s). This is a service to readers because it lets people know when things they might want to buy are available.

2. **Educational/informational:** Intended to educate or inform readers. This is a service to readers because the author has done the work of finding, filtering, and explaining the material in ways that are relevant to readers.

3. **Inspirational/entertaining:** Intended to motivate, support, encourage, and/or entertain readers. Sometimes we just need a kind word, empathy, or a distraction.

4. **Content curation:** Sharing curated content such as your own top posts or those of others, upcoming events, best recipes, etc. This is helpful for readers because it saves them time, reviews things they may have missed, and pre-filters content for importance or relevance.

5. **Community building:** Intended to encourage interaction and engagement among readers; these newsletters generally present a topic or question for discussion and encourage people to leave comments on social media, a website, or on the newsletter itself (only available in some newsletter systems).

Some newsletters do more than one of these things, but all do at least one of them. We'll talk about promotional newsletters in Chapter 16, but for now, if you're following the guidelines in this book, most of your newsletters will not be strictly promotional. Putting promotional newsletters aside, let's consider the other four alternatives.

Take a moment to ask yourself which of these might be of particular benefit to your readers. **Given what you know about where your readers are in the context of their potential work with you when they first arrive in your business, how could you provide value?** Which of these options align with your skills or interests and your personality?

- If you're a connector who loves to read, listen, and review, you might do well with content curation. For example, your newsletter might include book reviews, lists of recipes you recommend, or a roundup of upcoming community events.

- If setting the record straight or correcting misinformation is your style, educational newsletters may be just the thing. For example, you might send out a "what the news got wrong" message each week or a short video explaining a common misconception in each edition.

- If you see yourself as nurturing and encouraging, and if you know that many of your clients feel nervous or unprepared when it comes to the type of work you do, perhaps encouraging notes would be a real service. In this case, your newsletter may focus on stories or case studies demonstrating that change is possible or inspirational quotes and ideas to support people as they are experiencing challenging times.

Activity: Writing a statement of purpose

Add a short statement to your Newsletter Framework Worksheet about the purpose of your newsletter. This is for your own use and doesn't need to be perfectly worded or formatted. You can edit and update it as you go along. It helps to have a vision to keep you oriented.

While there are many things you could do with your newsletter, remember to keep this statement focused on what would be useful to your clients and aligned with your work and the time you have available to prepare your newsletter.

Examples

My newsletter's purpose is to:

- ...share upcoming events and resources local to [my area of the world] that might be helpful or of interest to current or future clients

- ... pass along thoughts and useful tidbits of information/links for people who are [describe your people]

- ... share a weekly recipe that's easy to make, healthy, local, and seasonal

- ... share a weekly playlist (or photo or journal prompt or...) to help [my people] [describe how]

- ... provide encouragement, resources, and hope for those [working on their first website, experiencing chronic pain, struggling with parenting after adoption]

- ... bring a moment of lightness, levity, or inspiration to people going through a divorce

- ... educate people who live in [my area] about the [local flora/fauna, eating locally, herbalism, yoga in our area, ecological living]

- ... inform readers about upcoming [herb walks, classes, workshops, client openings, podcast episodes, top social media posts]

Selecting newsletter sections

To get even more specific, you can think about how you might deliver the content of your newsletter. It is possible to address several of the options above by combining multiple newsletter blocks.

Newsletter "blocks" are essentially sections you could include in your newsletter. These are mix-and-match, meaning **you can choose one block or you can combine a few of them. I recommend no more than three blocks.** It's perfectly fine to have only one. (This doesn't include the bio, which we'll discuss in Chapter 8; as a sneak peek, you'll want a bio in every newsletter.)

Here are some block options:

- Long and/or academic essay

- Short essay/message/story

- Video (link)

- Podcast (link)

- Upcoming events

- Roundup list (best social media posts, things of interest this week)

- Recommendation list

- Recipe, song/playlist, or similar

- Quote or poem

- Book or podcast review

- Custom or whimsy block (what's happening in the garden, woods, or ecosystem; herbs in the news; kitten of the week, etc.)

- Bio (more on your bio in Chapter 8)

Select one to three blocks that would consistently help your readers and fulfill your promise/vision for your newsletter. **You're aiming for a newsletter that is helpful to your readers and that complements but does not replace the 1:1 work you do with clients.**

Pick blocks that fit your time available and interests as well. Many practitioners would love to write long academic articles at least once a month, but most of us won't have the time to do this alongside the other aspects of running a practice. If it's something you can't reasonably expect yourself to do in the time you have available, skip it! Err on the side of caution here.

Examples

My newsletter for practitioners always consists of:

- A short message – informational or inspirational – for people in a solo clinical practice

- A list of upcoming classes or programs I'm teaching

- A list of three recommendations/links that might be of interest to practitioners, although some are general interest (e.g., novels or recipes I've recently enjoyed)

Even more examples:

- Kendra Adachi's Lazy Genius newsletter occasionally includes a section called "What's Saving My Life Right Now."

- Kendra Payne from The Herbal Scoop has a newsletter called *What's the Tea Tuesday* and follows a structure she calls "1-2-3 Here's the Tea" (three updates, two products you'll love, one herb you should know).

- Marketing coach George Kao has a newsletter that involves sending out links to his top-performing social media posts across various platforms each week.

- Artist and author Austin Kleon's wildly popular weekly newsletter is a list of ten things he thought were worth sharing that week.

Adding whimsy and personality

The nice thing about your newsletter is that there are no strict rules about what a newsletter should be or what sections it must include.

For our purposes, your newsletter only needs to be:

1. Reflective of you and your work

2. Welcoming, useful, and/or supportive to the people you most want to help

3. Regularly sent out

That's it.

Adding a touch of whimsy or personality to your newsletter goes a long way to making it something people want to read. If color holds significant meaning to you, you're allowed to write a red-themed newsletter one month and an orange-themed newsletter the next. If calmness is a big part of your work and what you bring to the world, perhaps your recommendation section is called "3 things that helped me feel calm this week."

If you have a hobby or passion that's not directly related to your 1:1 work but that is a big part of who you are and how you see the world, it is okay to sprinkle that passion into your newsletter. It brings personality and gives your readers a better sense for who you are.

Examples

- Forest bathing guide Kristen Mastel is also the head librarian at the University of Minnesota Arboretum and shares photos and excerpts from rare books related to plants and natural history in her newsletter, along with upcoming forest bathing sessions and other tidbits focused on connecting people with nature.

- Herbalist Bonnie Rose Weaver sends out Whale Wednesday newsletters, noting that whales symbolize expansiveness and bring a lighthearted energy to their newsletter intended for city folks. Even though the newsletter content doesn't often directly relate to whales, Bonnie Rose believes that Whale Wednesdays are something everyone can celebrate.

- Many newsletter writers who are also music enthusiasts include a seasonal or thematic playlist in their newsletters; people who love cooking may include a few of the tastiest recipes they've tried recently.

Tips for choosing sections

- If you're having a hard time choosing, model your newsletter sections after those found in newsletters that resonates with you, and let it evolve from there. There's nothing wrong with borrowing section ideas from other people and tweaking them for yourself. (We're using these as inspiration and not borrowing specific words or phrases, of course!)

- If you think of a section that would be fun or useful or exciting to you – and you suspect that it might also be useful to your readers – give it a try.

- Remember, you're going for a newsletter-sized piece of content. In almost all cases, you'll have better results with a short, succinct newsletter. Stay focused on your promise to your reader. It's tempting to keep adding blocks and to take a "more is better" approach. People are skimming newsletters between other pieces of life.

- Most people don't succeed in writing/sending regularly because their newsletter vision is too involved. You'll set yourself up for procrastination and fizzling if your eyes are bigger than your stomach when you're planning your newsletter.

- It is okay to factor in and even to prioritize what interests you and how you like to communicate. What would it look like if writing your newsletter was easy and fun?

Activity: Choosing your newsletter blocks

Time to make some decisions. Fill in the final portion of your Newsletter Framework Worksheet by recording the block(s) you've chosen, along with a few notes about your vision for the block. Be as specific as you can since this will make the writing process easier. Will you have a title for each section? If so, note your title idea(s) here.

Takeaways and next steps

- You don't have to write a long or heavily researched essay for each newsletter (although you can!).

- Think about the types of newsletters you like to receive and aim to create a newsletter your readers like to receive.

- Short and succinct newsletters tend to work best.

- Select one to three newsletter "blocks" based on your own interests and what would serve your readers.

- Consider adding a touch of whimsy or personality into one or more of your blocks.

- Your newsletter should complement but not replace the 1:1 work you do with clients.

Newsletter Tip: Having more than one type of newsletter

You may be wondering whether your newsletter should follow the same format every time you send. Some people like having different types of newsletters: For example, you might prefer to send a meditation out on the new moon and an essay out on the full moon. Or some writers send out a journal prompt on Mondays and a social media roundup on Fridays, each containing different newsletter blocks.

If you're new to writing newsletters and/or if your time is limited, I highly recommend sticking to just one type of newsletter (other than promotional pieces, which we'll discuss in Chapter 16), at least for now. Adding a second type of newsletter makes the writing and sending processes more complex, and it's easier to get overwhelmed or to forget what goes into each type of newsletter. If you want to add a second type of newsletter later, add it in after you've been consistent and feel like you're in a rhythm with the original version.

If you truly want to have multiple types of newsletters, then go through the process above with each type, identifying which sections will be included. In the next chapter, you'll also create separate templates for each type of newsletter. Remember to take into consideration both what you want to send and what your readers might like to receive.

If you have multiple types of newsletters, you'll want them to have a coherent feel so that it's clear they are both coming from you and they feel related. I recommend using the same fonts, colors, salutation, sign-off, headings, and logo/bio placement in all versions of your newsletter (more on this in Chapter 8).

Chapter 7

Create a Writing Template

Now that you've decided on the sections you'll use in your newsletter, the next step is to codify your sections so that you'll remember what to do when it's time to write. Consistency in your content and format will allow you to write your newsletter more quickly. When your newsletters have a predictable format, this also creates a sense of safety and connection with your readers. If the format changes every time you send, it can be disconcerting and more difficult for readers to associate your content with the work you do.

To make things easier, we'll create templates you can use each time you sit down to write and send your newsletter.

Separate writing from formatting

Writing your newsletter and formatting/scheduling it are two separate processes. Both can be stressful, in their own special ways.

Your life will be easier if you separate these into two distinct tasks.

I recommend separating writing from formatting and scheduling by a day or two (or more), but if that doesn't work, give yourself at least a few hours between writing and scheduling.

I don't recommend writing your newsletter directly in your newsletter software (MailerLite, Mailchimp, etc.) for several reasons:

- If you write in your newsletter software, it's easy to get distracted or frustrated by the formatting, trying to remember how to add images, etc.

- It's better to have the content of your newsletter stored outside your newsletter software. If you lose access to the newsletter software, you will still have copies of your writing.

- If you write in the platform that you usually use for writing other things, your brain will settle into writing more easily.

Since you're separating writing from formatting, you'll want two templates: one in your writing software (your writing template) and one in your newsletter software (your sending template). We'll start by creating your writing template in this chapter. In Chapter 8, we'll work on creating a sending template.

Don't start from a blank page

Once you've decided on a format, creating a template to work from each time you write a newsletter can make all the difference. Rather than staring at a blank page each time you sit down to write, you'll have a framework to fill in. Having a writing template will also remind you of which sections go into your newsletter and provides the opportunity to add thoughts and notes to the document throughout the week/month.

Choose writing software that's familiar

Pick writing software to use. Many people choose Google Docs or Word, although feel free to use whatever you usually use for writing projects. **Choose something that's dedicated to word processing, that has automatic backup, and that you know how to use/find.**

Use this program to create a basic document that includes each section of your newsletter. You can add a reminder about what goes into each section if you think you're liable to go off topic. This template only includes sections that will change from one newsletter to the next. Your writing template does not need to include visual features like your logo, your signature/sign-off, or anything else that stays consistent with each issue.

Your template will likely be *very* simple. It may only contain a few words. It may look so simple, in fact, that it doesn't seem worth using.

Having your newsletter outlined when you sit down to write will make a difference both in how easy it is to write your newsletter and in how consistent your newsletter feels to its readers.

Example template

Here's the template I work from each week:

Subject line:

Hi there.

[My main message goes here.]

Take care,

Camille

Upcoming

- *Add three things here*

Recommendations

- *Add three things here*

It seems ridiculous that a basic template like this would make a difference, but it does. When I sit down to write each week, I fill in each of these spots in whichever order I like. Sometimes I add in recommendations throughout the week so they're ready to go when it's time to write.

The reminder of which sections I include and the fact that I'm not starting from a blank page keeps me on track and makes the writing process feel manageable.

Working from a template also means that the fonts, icons, and sections remain consistent from week to week, which is a small but symbolically important signal of consistency and predictability.

Adapt your template over time

Once you pick a format and create a template, you might find that adjustments are needed. This is fine.

Keep your eye on newsletters you receive from other people. Now that you're writing your own newsletter, you'll likely have a keener interest in how others are structuring their newsletters, how often they're sending, etc.

If you notice a structure or format in someone else's newsletter that you think might apply to yours, feel free to borrow it. Many people have borrowed and modified the format I use over the years, and I'm happy that it's provided some inspiration.

You can add or remove sections or make subtle changes to your template at any point. You're aiming for a format that works for you, that reflects positively on your work, and that will be well-received by your readers.

In summary, don't feel locked in once you create a template. This isn't a permanent decision, and you can adjust as you go along.

Copy your writing template immediately

In the next chapter, we'll discuss moving your newsletter content from the writing template to a sending template.

After adding one newsletter to your ESP/sending template, I recommend immediately making a copy of the current newsletter (or the writing template itself) to prepare for the next newsletter. If you have thoughts for or additions to your next newsletter before you're ready to write, you can dump them into the waiting draft document without worrying about formatting or precise wording. When it's time to write, your ideas, thoughts, and links will be waiting for you.

Activity: Create your writing template

Create your own writing template in whatever software you'll be using to write your newsletter. Include any notes on how you'll format the subject line, the key sections you'll include, and your greeting and sign-off.

Note that you technically do not need to include the greeting and sign-off here as they don't usually change each time you write a newsletter, but I find it helpful to include them so that I have a feel for the full effect of my message as I'm writing.

Add your template or check it off on your Newsletter Framework Worksheet.

Takeaways and next steps

- Create a basic writing template in a writing software such as Word, Notion, or Google Docs.

- The template will contain key headings for your newsletter, including blank spaces to fill in for each section or block you'll include in each newsletter.

- Make a copy of your writing template after sending each newsletter. Add new ideas, links, and other material to the fresh template throughout the week or month.

Chapter 8

Create a Sending Template

In addition to your writing template, you'll also want to have a sending template in your newsletter software (MailerLite, Kit/ConvertKit, etc.) so you're not starting from scratch with formatting each time your newsletter goes out.

The point of using a template within your newsletter software is to **avoid spending time worrying about how your newsletter looks each time you send one.** You'll pick a format, stick with it, and cut/paste your content from your writing template into this template within your newsletter software.

Use the simplest possible format

I don't recommend using one of the pre-made templates your newsletter service likely offers. Instead, you want something *simple* that feels like you.

Most people make the mistake of over-formatting a newsletter. Aim for clear and easy rather than fancy.

Unless you have extensive experience in graphic design, your newsletter will almost certainly become increasingly weirder the fancier you try to make it. Even if you use pretty pre-made templates and even if you have a vague sense that you should "brand" your newsletter.

The second you try to change almost anything on a pre-made template, the whole thing starts to look a bit off.

Remember, the point of your newsletter is to connect with your readers and to share a bit about you and your work. Hiding behind a formal/branded template may make you seem less relatable and more commercial. Additionally, the more complex your formatting gets, the more time it will take to format and send your newsletters.

Instead, my recommendation is to keep your template as visually simple as possible. Aim for a newsletter with plenty of open space that's easy to read.

Camille's Formatting Guidelines

- White background, dark grey or black font

- Font size at least 12- to 14-point

- Do not include images other than a small logo and a headshot (both optional) unless they are needed to illustrate a concept in your newsletter

- Left justify your text

- Use official headers (H1, H2, H3) to differentiate sections

- Avoid borders around the message, but do use dividers to separate sections

Caveat: I'll remind you here, again, that **you are welcome to ignore my suggestions if you like.** Some people love and use heavily branded, visually complex emails with excellent results. Business coach Leonie Dawson shared about trying out a simple newsletter written as a "normal" email and found that it didn't feel like them at all. They went right back to sending colorful and graphic-rich emails and haven't looked back. (Do note that Leonie is exceptionally talented when it comes to visuals!)

Background colors

It may seem like a good idea to use your brand colors as a background in your newsletter. This is probably not a good idea. It may make your text hard to read and doesn't look the same on all devices. **People who have visual challenges, color blindness, and so forth may not be able to read your text if the background color and font color are similar or if certain colors are used together.** Stick with a white background and a very dark-colored font for increased accessibility: Grey or black font are preferred for this.

Avoid borders

You almost certainly do not need borders in your newsletter. They don't always show up properly on mobile devices, and they can be harsh on the eyes if not done properly. They're also just one more thing to worry about when you're formatting. If you truly think you need a border around a section or around your entire newsletter, you're welcome to give it a try, but please ask someone for feedback and be sure to have a look at your newsletter on mobile, tablet, and full-screen views before sending. If you don't feel strongly about it, skip the border.

Fonts

Pick an easy-to-read font for the body of your messages. Typically, sans serif fonts are easier to read in the body of an email than serif fonts, although there are exceptions to this rule. The font size should be at least 12-point, although 14-point may work better for some fonts. When in doubt, go for increased readability – especially if many of your potential clients are middle–aged or beyond!

For headlines, you can get a bit creative with your fonts. If you have branded fonts on your website, you can use the same ones in your newsletter if they are common fonts accessible on most computers. If you use a fancy/paid font in your newsletter, it may not come through on the reader's device if they don't have the font installed.

You can usually change the settings in your newsletter software so that all headings use the same font/color. Do this to make your life easier.

If you don't yet have fonts picked out for your brand, you can use Fontjoy or similar websites to select fonts that pair well together. Select one font to use for headers within your emails and one to use for the body of your email.

Left justify your text

If you're tempted to center the text in your newsletter for a bit of aesthetic flare, please rethink that decision.

It's okay to center text when it's a short bit of copy that's meant to stand out. Examples include headlines, quotes, or brief testimonials. Longer pieces of writing should be left justified for several reasons.

For example, here is a paragraph that is centered instead of left-justified:

Left justification is easier to read, makes your newsletter look more visually appealing and professional, and is more accessible for readers who have visual impairments or dyslexia. Another important consideration is that centered text may not display properly on some smaller devices and in some email clients due to differences in the way these devices interpret coding. On smaller devices like cell phones, centered text can mean that the reader will need to scroll left to right to view all your content – and many folks are unlikely to do this.

Now read the same paragraph in a left-justified format:

Left justification is easier to read, makes your newsletter look more visually appealing and professional, and is more accessible for readers who have visual impairments or dyslexia. Another important consideration is that centered text may not display properly on some smaller devices and in some email clients due to differences in the way these devices interpret coding. On smaller devices like cell phones, centered text can mean that the reader will need to scroll left to right to view all your content – and many folks are unlikely to do this.

It's much easier to read the second way, isn't it? The longer the paragraph, the more difficult it is to read when it's centered.

Images

Using images in your newsletter means longer load time, a higher chance that your newsletter will get categorized as spam, and more time on your end fiddling with formatting, finding an open-access image, adding a caption and alternate text (alt text), etc.

Unless you need an image to illustrate a point, don't use one. (Exception: If you're sending a video as part of your newsletter, you might wish to include a screenshot of the video that's linked to YouTube or similar.)

If you do use an image that is important for understanding the message in your newsletter, please take the time to add alt text. This is descriptive text that is displayed if images are disabled or not working or read in place of the image for people who are using screen readers.

Headers

Headers are the titles or labels at the top of sections in a document or webpage. They help organize content, making it easier to read and find information quickly. They're particularly important for people who are using a screen reader to read your newsletter.

It's tempting to create a header by manually making the font bigger, making it bold, and/or using a different font or color. Rather than doing this, please use the official headers (H1, H2, H3) to make your newsletter more accessible to those using screen readers. There should only be one Heading 1 (H1), which is the title of your newsletter.

Heading 2 (H2) is used for major subsections, while Heading 3 (H3) is for subsections within an H2 section, etc.

Colors

You might think that without using colors liberally in your newsletter, it won't be branded enough. This isn't the case at all! While black/grey on white is recommended for the body font/background, you can change the color of the links or headers. **Do make sure that the header colors are dark enough to stand out on a white background and keep the colors the same in each newsletter.** Otherwise, stick to the basics. Aim for the feel of writing a personal note to the reader.

Logo

You have the option of using a logo at the top of your newsletter. This is not required, but if you have a logo and want to use it, this is the place. I recommend centering the logo (instead of right/left justify) and including a link to your homepage. When you add a link to your logo, have it open in a new tab. Usually there is a box to check to make this happen.

Your signature and bio

While most of your newsletters are not overtly promotional, it is helpful to remind people who you are, what you do, and how to work with you in your signature. **I recommend including a small headshot along with a one- to two-sentence bio emphasizing who you help/what you help them do and linking to your primary service(s).**

Most newsletter software includes the option to include a signature block that includes a headshot, biographical info, and links to your social media account(s).

Creating a one- to two-line description of what you do and who you help is outside the scope of this book, but some general advice is to be specific, write about who you help and what you help them do, and include a specific link to work with you. I think it's helpful to include one or two humanizing/whimsical pieces of information.

Here are a few sample templates to consider. Don't hesitate to modify heavily or discard these entirely and create your own.

- [Your name] helps [people who you help] do [whatever transformation you offer]. [Your name] [add a fact or two]. You can sign up for an [appointment, discovery call, package] here.

- Hi. I'm [your name]. I offer [the thing you offer] for [people you help] who want to [change you work toward]. I [add something related and interesting]. I have openings for new clients in [month]. To learn more or to schedule a [discovery call, appointment, package] click here. I'd love to work with you.

- I'm [your name]. I work with [people you work with]. When you're ready, there are [x] ways I can help you [make the change you help with]: 1) [short phrase with link], 2) [short phrase with a link]. (This signature is modeled on Justin Welsch's in his weekly newsletter.)

A photo is helpful as it humanizes you; we are generally better at remembering faces, and again, one of the goals of the newsletter is for people to remember you when they need you. If you don't love being in photos, you can skip it. If you decide to use a photo, use one where you can see your face (no sunglasses or hats that shade your face). A casual photo is fine. Ask yourself whether the photo reflects the business values you want to project. If not, take another one.

Example: my newsletter signature

Hi there! I'm Camille Freeman. I've been in practice as a nutritionist and herbalist since 2004, with a focus on fertility and menstrual health. Now, I mostly focus on helping other practitioners. I'm writing a book about newsletters. I also homeschool two kiddos and spend a ton of time reading [link to my bookshop.org reading list]. I do 1:1 mentoring [link] and offer courses and programs for practitioners [link]. I think you're great.

Activity: Create a sending template

Log in to your ESP and create a template with the elements above. Set up the headers, fonts, colors, logo, signature/bio, and any other thematic elements you're choosing to include. If your ESP doesn't offer the option to create a template or if it's outside your capacity to create a template right now, you can also create a regular newsletter using the settings you've chosen. The next time you send a newsletter, you can duplicate/copy the existing one and replace the text as needed.

Note that creating a template in your ESP can be a time-consuming endeavor. The simpler your template is, the less time it will take to create it! Also, feel free to work on your template one step at a time, spreading the work out over several weeks.

How to use your templates

Now you have two templates: one in your writing software and one in your newsletter software.

Here's what to do:

1. Write your newsletter by filling in the blanks in your writing template.

2. Give it a day – or at least a few hours – to marinate.

3. Review and make any needed edits to the content.

4. Copy the content into your newsletter software template.

5. Send yourself a test email; verify that all links are working and that

the formatting looks okay on desktop and mobile.

6. Send your email or schedule it to go out at a future time.

7. Copy over a new/blank version of your writing template so you can add ideas and links to your next newsletter draft as you think of them.

Takeaways and next steps

- Create a sending template in your newsletter software.

- No images (other than logo and bio) unless specifically needed. Simple > fancy.

- White background. Dark font. 12-point or bigger.

- Include a short bio that shares who you work with, how you help them, and how to get started working together.

Newsletter Tip: Working with an assistant on your newsletter

Using the processes in this book has made it easier for me to work with an assistant to get my newsletter published each week (thanks, Amy!). The most important thing I do is write the newsletter, but I don't necessarily need to be the one who edits, formats, tests links, and gets the whole thing scheduled in MailerLite.

Our process is as follows:

- Every Tuesday, I write the newsletter in Upbase (our task and project management system).

- On Wednesday, Amy pastes the newsletter copy into our MailerLite template, sends a test email, checks links, schedules the newsletter send, and posts a copy of the newsletter on my website. *Note that I don't recommend posting a copy of your newsletter to your website when you're just getting started. See Chapter 14 for more information on this.*

- Amy also creates a fresh writing template for me to work from the following week. Any upcoming events that carry over from one week to the next are left in the template.

- Thursdays at 8:15 a.m. the newsletter goes out to subscribers.

- We have recurring tasks set up in Upbase for each step listed above so we're on the same page as we move through the process each week.

I've included a video of how we use Upbase to do this on the book resources page: https://www.writebetterletters.com/resources.

Chapter 9

Coming Up with Ideas for Your Newsletter

You have your templates, you've thought carefully about your readers, and you have a good sense for the tone of your newsletter and the type of messages you'll send.

Now, it's time to write. If your newsletter will be a compilation of links or a new recipe each week, you may not need to do much beyond a bit of research. However, most of us include at least one short piece of writing in each newsletter, whether it's a description of the links we recommend, a short story or message, or a longer essay.

You've done some of the hard work already by choosing the sections to include in your newsletter. Next, we'll dive into the process of coming up with ideas for your newsletter.

Your perspective is important

It's easy to believe that your newsletter should be life-changing, groundbreaking, or encyclopedic. We put a lot of pressure on ourselves to create something profound each time we send.

Remember, though, that your readers typically experience your newsletters as disposable content. Newsletters are most often received as helpful and/or enjoyable but not crucial to making it through the day.

What matters to your reader is receiving a message of interest to them from you. Both the "of interest to them" and the "from you" parts are important.

Your thoughts, your perspective, the filters through which you see life and think about the world are important, particularly in the context of the work you do. This is what will draw your clients to you (and push the folks who aren't your people away from you). Pushing some folks away isn't a bad thing. You're writing specifically for the people with whom you want to work. Others may not find value in your newsletter, and that is okay.

Newsletters that work well to serve readers are often short and focused. They cover or address one small thing.

If your newsletter feels big and cumbersome, it probably is. We'll talk about this later.

For now, the first thing to do as you gather ideas for your newsletter is to start noticing what you see around you.

The deeper act of noticing

In Verlyn Klinkenborg's excellent book *Several Short Sentences About Writing*, he discusses the practice of noticing. Klinkenborg writes that most people believe that what they notice isn't important and have never learned how to truly notice things. He points out that we often assume other, more important people have "pre-noticed" the important things.

To write newsletters that matter both to you and to your readers, become an observer of the world around you. Be aware of what you notice, reflect on your noticings, and let ideas emerge from there.

What you notice is filtered through your own experience. Your noticings will be different than mine, and this is what will help make your newsletter distinctive.

Noticing is the first step, perhaps the precursor, to creating thoughts and work of your own.

To develop topics for your newsletter, practice bringing your noticings to the surface, giving them time and space and attention. See if they develop into something you'd like to share with readers.

Keep a list of what you notice

Maybe you notice a question frequently asked by clients, one you could reasonably answer in a one-to-many format.

Maybe you notice how you feel with the changing of the seasons, and you think about how that applies to your clients as well.

Or, on a walk, you begin thinking about how movement helps you feel better when you're having a hard day.

Once you know you'll be writing a newsletter, you can be on the lookout for topics that might be of interest to you and to your readers.

You'll find that these ideas begin to arrive at unusual times.

Much of what you have to offer is in the perspective you bring. **It's not about the content, it's about how you, the writer, interpret and understand and contextualize the world.** It's difficult to philosophize while you're sitting in front of your computer trying to think of something useful to say.

Instead, **I recommend keeping a small notebook with you or having a special place on your phone (many people use the Notes app) to jot down any ideas or noticings that cross your mind as you're out and about.**

Practice diffuse thinking

Barbara Oakley, author and educator behind the popular and free online course, *Learning How to Learn*, encourages students to know the difference between focused thinking and diffuse thinking.

Focused thinking occurs when you turn your mind specifically to a task. For example, drafting your newsletter or researching topic ideas both require focused thinking. Diffuse thinking happens when you turn away from the topic at hand and do something else, often something repetitive that doesn't require focused attention – like taking a walk, showering, cooking, knitting or other crafts, etc. Your brain works differently during these times, connecting ideas in unexpected ways or coming up with solutions that may not have been obvious before.

While it can be helpful to spend some focused time thinking about your newsletter content or topic ideas, if you find that you're stuck or can't come up with any ideas, it may help to turn to diffuse thinking instead.

It's not uncommon to have a brilliant(ish) idea when you're walking the dog, taking a shower, or lying down to sleep. Record these ideas in a notebook or a special place on your phone/computer. The ideas you write down don't need to be fleshed out fully. Any little tidbit you notice is fair game.

- Something that catches your eye or your imagination on your morning walk

- A question asked by a client or colleague

- A social media post or other content being passed around that you'd like to build on or discuss

- Quotes from books, movies, songs that you find inspiring or meaningful

- Something new you learned or changed your mind about

Any of these are potential fodder.

You'll find that many of the ideas you write down are not actually that great when you return to them later. A substantial portion of them will be indecipherable. This is okay. **The more ideas you write down, the more ideas you'll have.**

When it's time to write, you can either pick something that's been on your mind lately or you can look at your list of newsletter ideas for inspiration. Sometimes I find that there's a message I've been dying to get off my chest all week, and other times, I look at my running list and pick something that seems interesting or fun to me in the moment.

(If you truly run out of ideas, you can use Appendix 1 to rustle up a few things to write about.)

Activity: Start your idea list

Get a notebook or determine which app/platform you'll use to jot down your topic ideas. Write down at least five ideas for newsletter topics, even if you don't think they're very good ones. Pin, bookmark, or otherwise save this list somewhere you'll be able to access easily when an idea strikes.

Takeaways and next steps

- Look for inspiration from daily life: client questions, the natural world, personal experiences.

- Keep a running list of topic ideas and things you notice.

- Don't filter ideas on your list; add anything that strikes your fancy.

- As you begin to notice your ideas, you will have more of them.

Newsletter Tip: Saying the wrong thing/offending people

When you're clear about what your newsletter offers and when you're writing specifically to the people who you most want to work with as clients, your list will start to fill up with people who are genuinely interested in you and your work. Even so, sharing parts of yourself can feel quite vulnerable. Many newsletter writers worry about inadvertently offending readers.

If this is something that worries you, remember that your newsletter readers are predisposed to appreciate your work. These are not random strangers on the internet, but rather people who have heard about your work and liked what they saw enough to share their email address with you.

Imagine this: You attend a talk at the library about creating sustainable garden beds and enjoy the presenter's energy. Although you don't have garden space now, you may be getting access to a community garden plot later this year, so you sign up for the presenter's email list to stay in touch. You find 80 percent of this person's newsletters helpful and relevant, while 20 percent of them don't quite land with you or are promoting services you don't need until you have access to garden space.

I suspect that your response upon receiving the 20 percent of emails that don't resonate with you is not to think to yourself, "Ugh, this person is terrible, and they're bothering me. Let me unsubscribe immediately."

Unless the message is egregiously bad – something far outside your values – you are likely to give the person the benefit of the doubt if they publish something that doesn't resonate with you or with which you disagree. You simply delete that message and move on with your life.

The same will be true of your readers. If you say something "wrong" or your message doesn't come across as you'd intended it to, most of your readers will simply delete the message or assume that you may have misspoken. Sometimes people will unsubscribe, and that's okay, too.

Should you avoid controversial topics in your newsletter? Not necessarily. I don't recommend avoiding these topics if they are relevant to your clientele and if you have something to say. If you feel strongly about a topic and you are sharing it to be of service to your readers, go ahead and include it.

You may lose some people, and that's fine.

On the other hand, it's best to stick to your lane when it comes to controversial topics that you don't have some level of expertise on and/or that do not directly affect your practice or potential clients.

For example, presidential elections, wars/conflicts, politics in general, and vaccines are all hot button topics. **These are important issues that may affect you personally, your clients, and/or your community, and it's okay to put them in your newsletter if you filter through the lens of being of service to your readers.**

If you're raising money for Palestine or want to share a study about the efficacy of vaccines, please feel free to share these things if they are relevant and of interest to your readers as well.

Remember that you and your business are two separate entities. Keep your business's mission and values in mind when you're deciding what to share.

You are not a news outlet, and you are not obliged to personally put out a statement on every hot button topic of the day.

Chapter 10
Filtering Your Topic Ideas

Once you start writing down ideas, you'll find that your newsletter topic list begins to snowball. Your noticings and your ideas will flow more readily.

Not all ideas will be appropriate for newsletters, though.

You may have thoughts on your topic list that apply to your personal life, to your other interests and hobbies, or to life in general.

To decide whether an idea would make a good newsletter topic, ask yourself if it is something that directly applies to your clients, your work, or to serving your community in general. **Sharing ideas, stories, or other content indiscriminately risks making the newsletter about you rather than about your reader.**

The purpose of the newsletter is to serve the reader in some small way. To make sure you're doing that, run any content – especially stories – through this filter:

How does this content, idea, or story relate to or help the person reading it?

Your content doesn't need to be deep and profound.

It doesn't necessarily need to change the reader's life dramatically.

However, there should be a point to what you're sharing. If you find yourself including a story only because you want to tell it, set it aside for now.

Providing specific advice may backfire

When you're writing a newsletter to build your 1:1 practice, the idea is to serve your readers and demonstrate your work, philosophy, and/or vision so that folks who are potentially interested in working together can decide if you're a good fit.

It's easy to think that you should demonstrate your training and expertise by making suggestions such as "here's who should take XXX herb/supplement and what dose to use" if you're a nutritionist or "10 things you can do to improve your website copy" if you're a copywriter. The first thing many of us think about when asked to write something that serves the reader is providing educational content. Your intention may be to share something with readers that they don't already know and to provide concrete, actionable steps.

There are several reasons I don't recommend doing this if your goal is to bring in more 1:1 clients.

First, you likely do not have the time or space in your newsletter to provide enough information for your readers to make an informed decision or to learn how to do the thing on their own. If you're providing any sort of healthcare or healthcare-adjacent services, it's an ethical grey area to make blanket recommendations without providing a full list of contraindications, interactions, indications, etc.

If you're in another business, your readers may or may not have the expertise to apply your advice since you don't know their baseline knowledge and experience level.

There are very few pieces of advice that will apply universally to all readers.

Second, the people you're writing to are your potential clients. These are typically not people who are trying to DIY their healthcare (or their website or their content or whatever else you offer). The people who want to work with you are those who value and want guidance from someone with training and experience.

Third, it requires a lot of time to do this well. You are not a professional newsletter writer. Your value is not in your encyclopedic knowledge of herbs, supplements, copywriting, etc. You aren't here to replace Wikipedia with your newsletter. Writing textbook-style essays most likely isn't a good use of your time and doesn't showcase your particular approach to the work you do or build relationships with your readers.

Identify the main idea

The easiest way to make sure you aren't accidentally giving unhelpful advice to your newsletter readers is to ask yourself one question after you've written your draft (or, better yet, before you write your draft):

What is the point of this piece?

Summarize your main point in a single sentence. What do you want the reader to take away from what you've written?

If you aren't sure about your point or if the point you're making is too broad or better suited to a 1:1 conversation, here are some ideas to consider instead.

Idea 1: Get more granular

If your answer is "Consider taking echinacea to support your immune system," you may want to rework things. This is specific advice and not a case that can be made in a newsletter-sized piece of writing.

Instead of centering your thesis around a large topic and blanket advice, can you illustrate a smaller, related point?

For example, if you want to write about echinacea, consider writing about variations in quality of echinacea products and why it matters. Tell a story about the time you sampled your friend's 10-year-old echinacea tincture, which tasted like grain alcohol, and why it probably wasn't doing anything for her.

The main idea of this revised essay might be: It's important to buy or make high-quality preparations or you're likely to waste your money and not notice any results. Or it might be: Here's how to tell if your echinacea tincture is of good quality.

Idea 2: Motivate or stimulate thought rather than educate

Another question to consider: Is your goal necessarily to educate? It's sometimes more helpful to encourage or motivate readers or to ask questions rather than provide answers.

If your original topic was why magnesium can be an excellent supplement (advice!), could you pivot to a discussion of how it's easy to rely on supplements and bypass more profound changes to food and lifestyle? Or discuss the fear that comes up when we read about how nutrients are being depleted in the soil and how you navigate this both personally and with clients?

Idea 3: Make it personal

Instead of summarizing textbooks or "the research" on a topic, share something that's filtered through your own lens. Why does this matter *to you*? What do you think about it? You don't need to provide a full background story. You can simply say: "A lot of people think x about y, but I think z. Here's why I care so much." Share your perspective, a small insight you've had on the topic, or something you've learned from your work in this area.

Include personal stories with care

You don't have to include stories in your newsletter. You can have a wonderful newsletter that rarely or never includes stories from your life. However, if you have a good story to illustrate a point or to draw the readers into the newsletter, I recommend using it.

You don't necessarily need to get into your postpartum perineal care routine or the details of your divorce. A small story of how a plant is important to you, the first time you met a teacher or mentor, a common misconception and how it affects your work are all very effective in sharing bits of yourself with readers without overdoing it.

If you want to include a story, you'll want to condense it down to its most essential parts. Your readers don't need a full backstory on each person you mention. Give just enough detail to make your point. Leave room for the reader to breathe their own life into your words rather than filling in the blanks for them.

Stories that relate to your life can also work well – for example, the feeling of being rundown after an exhausting week caring for a loved one or grief after the loss of a pet if you can relate it back to a word of advice or encouragement for your readers.

You can start with a story you've noticed and ask yourself: What's the point? **Why is this meaningful to me, and why might it matter to my reader?**

Things you notice are for a reason; your perspective, what you notice, is inherently "you" – which is what we're getting at. **But remember to apply the filter. Not everything you notice needs to be shared with or wedged into your newsletter. Some noticings are for you alone.** They represent beauty, depth, etc. in other ways and may be more appropriate to share with a friend or in your journal.

Considerations when mentioning others

When you mention someone else in your newsletter, whether it's a family member, friend, colleague, or client, you'll want to think carefully about the ethics of doing so.

Some writers are eminently comfortable sharing highly personal details. Others prefer not to let it all hang out online. There's a spectrum, and you get to show up wherever you are along the spectrum. **It is possible to tell stories that convey a point without feeling as if you're sharing intimate details of your life with readers.**

Some writers find that they get better engagement by sharing stories relating to interactions with a spouse/partner, children, clients, etc. While posts about relationship strife, silly things your children have said, or a conflict you had at the store with a neighbor may get more clicks, opens, readers, etc., we need to consider the possible cost.

Here are some questions that may help you filter any stories involving other people:

- Do you have consent to share this information?

- Is this sharing appropriate in a professional context?

- Is there a specific reason to share this story beyond increasing readership?

- If the other person/people involved in this story were reading my newsletter, would I feel uncomfortable with it?

- Does this story reflect me in the way I'm hoping to portray myself to my potential clients?

I recommend getting permission if anyone in your newsletter is recognizable (e.g., you'll be using their names or other identifying details) or anonymize the story so that it wouldn't be possible to figure out who you're discussing.

Sharing client stories

If you're in practice, you may find yourself wanting to share stories of things that have happened with your clients. Maybe they've had a great success you'd like to share, but maybe you made a big mistake or learned something in a different way. Is it okay to share these in your newsletter?

In general, if you anonymize the situation, it is likely okay to share the story. If you are bound by HIPAA, you'll likely want to avoid this or consult a lawyer about what might be doable in your situation.

Even though you technically can share client stories in your newsletter (in many cases), please think carefully about whether you want to do so. Our newsletters are about building relationships and strengthening community. How might your client feel if they see themselves in your newsletter, particularly if it could be construed in a negative light? Is there any chance they would feel exploited or uncomfortable with what you're sharing? Might it damage your relationship or the way they view the time spent with you? Might potential clients see this story and feel reluctant to work with you because they wouldn't be comfortable with their story being shared in this way?

If you want to use a client story, I'd recommend asking the client first, letting them know that you'll anonymize their name or leave it out altogether and the reason you want to share it. Give them full permission to opt out – remembering that you're in a position of power over them if you have ongoing work together and that this has the potential to damage your relationship. If you get permission, people may be quite excited about being featured in your newsletter, but it's important to have a choice.

If you want to share a client story or a story that even peripherally involves a client, I recommend first waiting a good deal of time, anonymizing the story, and/or combining several stories. "Clients often do this, which is when I do that." Rather than "My client Rachel once asked me..."

What you don't want is a client reading what you've written with a sinking feeling in their stomach or to leave anyone feeling vaguely icky and manipulated. Think about how you'd feel and proceed accordingly.

Your perspective is valuable

When evaluating your list of topic ideas, you might find that you're quick to dismiss almost everything you write down. Instead of being inspired by what you see out in the world – the art, the garden, other newsletters, ideas from books or conversations or lectures – you find yourself choosing not to write about these things because the idea has already been "taken."

You may read something so perfectly put that there's nothing more for you to say. You'll think to yourself, "I should just have everyone read this piece instead of trying to write my own." Or you see something beautiful and meaningful on a hike and think that you'll never be able to describe it in a way that resonates with someone else.

Which can lead to a spiral of depression and a lack of confidence.

Never think that because someone else has already "covered" something in their writing, article, newsletter, video, etc. your perspective doesn't matter.

You have a certain way of speaking, a view, and a timing that does matter. The way you say something may hit home for some readers in a way that other pieces have not.

Sometimes a slight change in one word, an added metaphor, fortuitous timing, or simply hearing the message from someone you trust versus someone you don't know can make all the difference. Other times, the message may be common knowledge to you but new to your readers.

I'm sure you've had this happen before: You've heard about concepts or had them explained to you repeatedly, but you never really "got" them until one person said it in a different way or until the time was just right for you to hear the message.

If a topic feels important or relevant to you, don't hesitate to address it yourself. There are likely people reading your newsletter who need to hear it from you.

If you come across content created by someone else that's profound or interesting, you absolutely can link to it in your message. But do it from a place of lifting someone else up rather than putting yourself down. Whenever we celebrate someone else, it can be validating in general.

If you decide to add to or address content that's been created by someone else, don't worry about being derivative. **It is 100% okay and even affirming and helpful to build on the work of others.** If someone said something that resonates with you and you'd like to add your own take to it, feel free to write about that topic. You can acknowledge where the inspiration came from and even quote the person or share their work.

Your words, your ideas, and your filter will add something to the topic.

The caveats here are to give credit where it's due and not to borrow large sections that aren't your own writing. We are going for "you" – not generic content, remember?

Activity: Practice combining ideas

I have a theory that if you deeply know your readers, you can find a relevant message from almost any story, item, or noticing. To play with this idea a bit, here's an exercise I like to do. Take anything from your desk or any object in sight and ask how it might relate to your readers. What story could you tell about this object to convey a point or an idea that would serve your readers?

Takeaways and next steps

- Filter your newsletter ideas by asking what would be helpful for your readers.

- Avoid providing specific advice in a one-to-many format.

- Make sure you can clearly identify the point or thesis of your writing.

- While educational pieces can be helpful, you can also encourage, motivate, or entertain in your writing.

- If you share stories, make sure they are concise and of value to your readers.

- Respect privacy and ethics when mentioning other people in your newsletter.

- Your perspective is important; you can add value to a topic by sharing your ideas, thoughts, or experiences.

Newsletter Tip: Sharing other people's work

It is always okay to link to someone else's work if you'd like to share an article, image, recipe, post, etc. Some newsletters, in fact, are built almost entirely as compilations linking to other works. If this is in service to your readers, have at it. If you'd like to include someone else's content directly in your newsletter, things are a bit trickier.

Any works published more than one hundred years ago are in the public domain and can be used freely. Even if something is in the public domain, it is still courteous and helpful to your readers to cite it and to link to the original source where possible. If you'd like to share a poem, a passage, or another piece of content but aren't sure if it's in the public domain, please do a search to find out. You can share an excerpt of a copyrighted work for education or critique without worrying about copyright infringement, as this falls under the fair use doctrine. However, it's important to use only the portion necessary to make your point and to provide proper attribution.

Please, please **don't grab an image off the web and use it without first checking to see if it's in the public domain or available to use under a Creative Commons license.** Use websites such as Pixabay and Pexels to find images that are not copyrighted. You can use your own images or search for images that are published with a Creative Commons license. (Most search engines have a checkbox to filter for this, although it is always a good idea to double check.)

Even when attribution isn't required, I always prefer to credit the author/artist and link to their work whenever possible. This helps build your ecosystem and create a feeling of mutualism rather than extraction.

Activity: Sharing other people's work

If you do share someone else's idea or writing, please consider letting them know. Tag them on social media if relevant or send a short email letting them know you appreciated their [message, post, etc.] and that you've built on it in your own newsletter this week, providing a link if you can. Creating content and sharing your ideas can be isolating and challenging; receiving a message like this can make someone's day and give them a needed boost to keep going. It also helps build community and increase awareness of your work.

Chapter 11

Writing a First Draft

We've talked about what to write about, but what does it look like to sit down and start writing?

First, you need to understand the difference between writing and editing. **Writing is expressing your thoughts on paper (or pixel). It doesn't matter how grammatically correct you are or if you use exactly the right words.** You're simply trying to get your ideas down so they're not living in your head.

Editing is revising your work for clarity, coherence, and quality so that your message comes through to the readers. While writing is a largely creative process, editing is more analytical.

Often, as you're writing, you'll realize that what you thought you understood about the topic is not actually what you think. You will change your mind, clarify your understanding (or at least identify murkiness), and develop your thinking as you go.

Newsletters are what business coach George Kao refers to as "level one" content – they're ideas in progress that you're testing out. These are not meant to be a complete compendium of any topic or idea. **They're small bits of content intended to be helpful, thought-provoking, and/or encouraging to your readers.**

When writing a first draft of a newsletter, your intention is to simply get your ideas down onto the page. Try to avoid editing as you write so you can stay in a creative frame of mind. Don't worry about grammar or the red squiggles on your document for now.

Writer Anne Lamott is known for embracing a "shitty first draft," and you should feel free to write one of these. You are unlikely to write a perfect piece on your first try. **The best way I know to get a newsletter written is to get something down, usually something that's not very good, and to edit it afterward.**

To start your writing process, either create a draft based on an idea that's been popping around in your head lately or refer to your list of newsletter ideas. Write stream of consciousness for a while, getting at least a loose sense of your ideas down on paper or pixel. (See Appendix 1 if you're fresh out of ideas.)

Finding time to write

We put things off when we think they're hard, when we aren't used to doing them, or when we think we'll be "bad" at them.

You probably have other obligations that seem more urgent than writing your newsletter.

The newsletter won't work to bring in more 1:1 clients unless you write it.

Sometimes it helps with motivation to remember that **you've made an implied promise to the people who have subscribed. They are expecting to hear from you.** Of course, you are allowed to change your mind. Your newsletter is a free service, and you don't owe it to anyone. However, unless you've made a conscious choice to discontinue writing or to write on a different schedule, there is an energetic commitment to the people who have signed up. So, let yourself be motivated by the people who are waiting to hear from you and by the knowledge that what you have to say may be exactly what someone needs to hear today.

Pick a regular time to write

I highly recommend having a regular schedule for writing (e.g., every Tuesday or every new moon). Base your writing schedule on the sending schedule you set in Chapter 3. For example, if you plan to send your newsletter each month on the first Monday, you might choose to schedule in writing time during the last week of each month. If you're planning to send every Wednesday, perhaps you schedule time to write your newsletter each Monday.

If this type of scheduling doesn't fit with your obligations or your working style, the next best way to get yourself to make time for writing your newsletter is to write along with someone else.

Co-working is a fantastic way to write your newsletter. I host a free co-working session most weeks that you're welcome to attend to get this done. Details about co-working are available on the book resources page: https://www.writebetterletters.com/resources.

You can use a service like Focusmate, which offers the ability to schedule a work session with someone else at almost any time of day and has a very generous free plan, or you can set up times to co-work in person or online with a friend or colleague. While it doesn't seem like co-working would be more effective than simply working on your own, it truly makes a big difference – at least for many people.

If you find that you aren't writing your newsletter and can't make time for it using one of the above methods, you may need to lower the bar for now. Shorten your newsletter and/or decrease the frequency with which you send until it works for you.

Give yourself a writing window

Remember when we talked about newsletters as mostly disposable content? To run a 1:1 practice, you'll need to be doing other marketing activities (more on this in Chapter 15), working with your clients, taking care of admin like bookkeeping, website upkeep, etc. You likely do not have five to ten hours to devote to writing, editing, and formatting each newsletter.

Review your typical weekly or monthly schedule and identify how much time you think you can devote to each edition of your newsletter. Remember that you'll need time to write, edit, schedule, check links, and have a mild freakout for each newsletter.

In the beginning, it will take more time than usual to get a newsletter finished. As you get into the habit, you'll do this more quickly. You won't be fiddling as much with the format, you'll know what needs to happen to write, and it will flow more easily.

After you've gotten the hang of things, **I recommend giving yourself no more than 1 to 1.5 hours to write your newsletter and up to an additional 30 to 45 minutes on a separate day to edit, format, and schedule it.** If you're great at writing quick first drafts, you might find that it's better to flip this – spending 30 to 45 minutes writing a first draft one day and 1 to 1.5 hours on another day editing, formatting, and scheduling.

Example: my newsletter writing process

I write my newsletter every Tuesday. Much of my thinking about what I'm going to write happens during my morning dog walks. I usually let my mind drift. I'm not consciously trying to think of newsletter ideas, but subconsciously, I know that I'll be writing my newsletter later that day. Interesting things from the world around me will arise or I'll think about questions/clients I've worked with recently. I add any ideas to my list of notes in my phone or, if something feels like it needs to come out now, I bring it to my writing session.

While my newsletter took much longer at first, now I allot approximately 30 minutes in front of the computer on Tuesdays for newsletter writing. (This is separate from the process of formatting and testing it, which happens the following day.) Most of the time, this is about right. Some days, I write for 30 minutes, and the result isn't solid. I don't feel good about sharing it, and I start over. This happens a few times per year. Other times, I send anyway, even if it's not perfect.

There are times when I'm ill, traveling, or otherwise occupied and don't have even 30 minutes to write. When this happens, I'll either skip a week (about two times a year), re-share something I've written previously, or write a very brief message – maybe just a sentence or two.

Write at a regular, predictable time

Many people find that writing comes more easily once their brain is expecting to do it on a regular schedule. You'll find that as you notice things to write about, ideas begin to pop up more regularly. Your idea list will fill out, and your brain will become accustomed to writing at a specific time.

I think of this as a learned reflex. Your digestive system produces enzymes and saliva minutes or even hours in advance of when it knows you'll be eating. Similarly, you'll begin thinking through a slightly different lens when you know you'll be writing at a particular time, even if you aren't consciously trying to do so.

Interestingly, sometimes the newsletters I write under duress, when I have nothing to say and it feels like my writing is subpar are those that are best received.

As an example, one Tuesday I was stuck when it was time to start writing my newsletter. Nothing from my list of potential topics was calling to me, and my brain felt like mush after a few very busy weeks. My assistant was leaving town for a few days, and I needed to get a draft to her ASAP if I wanted help posting and formatting the newsletter that week.

I was scrolling through my email for ideas (nothing!) and finally decided to write a quick piece about my email signature, which I had changed a bit recently. Writing it took about 15 minutes – which was all I had by this point – and I thought about not sending it out at all because it didn't feel up to my normal standards.

What happened is that tons of people wrote back – more than any other newsletter I'd sent that year – to say how helpful they'd found the message.

This is why it makes sense to write and send regularly versus just when the muse strikes – because sometimes necessity really is the mother of invention. "Having" to write something and committing to sending a newsletter regularly, knowing that some will be good and some will be less good, and knowing that we can't always predict which things will be helpful for the reader means that we have the chance to experiment and play a bit.

Sending what felt to me like a suboptimal newsletter reminded me that my readers appreciate practical tips and that my folks are interested in the nuance of clinical practice – what do we say in our email signatures and in our "out of office" emails? – I wouldn't have thought that would be super interesting initially, but I've learned that it is, and I love talking about these things, so it's a win-win.

Another takeaway from this experience is that **time spent writing doesn't always correlate with the result.** Sometimes the most helpful and well-received newsletters are those we dash off quickly with little time and brainpower available, and sometimes the newsletters we spend weeks agonizing over and that we feel encompass important and life-changing insights will not resonate at all with our readers.

Writing a newsletter is a process of co-creation, and you can't experience it fully until you start sending newsletters regularly and paying attention to the feedback you're receiving.

Activity: Schedule your writing time

Realistically assess your calendar and commitments for the time when you'd like to send your next newsletter. How much time can you spend on your newsletter, given the other things on your schedule? Allott about two-thirds to three-fourths of that time to writing and the remaining time to formatting/testing/scheduling. So, if you have 2 hours (which is about the max I'd go), give yourself 1.5 hours to write (put it in your schedule!) and about 30 minutes to format/check links/test/schedule. **Add this time into your calendar now so it doesn't surprise you later.**

Leave space between writing and sending

I recommend leaving at least 24 hours between writing your newsletter, editing it, and adding it to your email sending platform.

This allows you some time to step away from your newsletter for a second review a day or so later.

It also separates the work of writing from the work of formatting, testing, and scheduling your newsletter. These tasks require distinct types of thinking, and it's far too easy to get your attention dragged away by a small formatting issue or resizing a photo when you write directly into your email software.

I write my newsletters on Tuesdays. On Wednesdays, they get added to MailerLite, we send a test email, check all the links, etc. And on Thursdays around 8:15 a.m., the newsletters are sent out.

You may find that you prefer to have more time between these phases, or you might find that you can combine the second two steps.

I like to get the newsletter ready to go the day before so it can go out at a consistent time each week. **People start to look for it at that time, and** the consistency makes a small but hopefully significant contribution to the feeling of trust and reliability that I'm working to build with my readers. I'm looking to convey that I take their attention seriously and that I'm committed to showing up regularly for them.

Takeaways and next steps

- When writing a first draft, just get your thoughts down. Don't filter or edit as you go.

- Give yourself 1 to 1.5 hours to write a draft of your newsletter and 30 to 45 minutes to edit/format it. (It may take longer at first!)

- Writing and editing/formatting your newsletter are two separate processes.

- Schedule a day or so (or at least a few hours) between writing and editing.

- Block time into your calendar now to write and edit/schedule your next several newsletters.

- Time spent writing doesn't always correlate with the quality of your newsletter.

- You've made a promise to people who signed up for your newsletter; make the time to follow through on it.

Newsletter Tip: Writing ahead or batching newsletters

You may have heard the advice to "batch" your newsletters – setting aside a full day to write four or five (or more!) newsletters in advance. Then, you can schedule them to drip out to your readers over time.

This is an efficient use of your time and can be useful if you know you have a big trip coming up or a particularly busy time on the horizon. For example, if you're expecting a baby, moving, or going through another major life transition that can be anticipated, having newsletters pre-written can be the difference between keeping your business bopping along or experiencing a major dip in income.

Unless there is a specific reason to do so, however, I generally advise against writing newsletters weeks or months in advance.

If you pre-write your newsletters, you run a few risks:

1. If your newsletter is scheduled far in advance, it may cover something that doesn't fit the mood when it finally does come out. For example, if you pre-write a message about how ideas are spewing forth like lava and celebrating volcanic energy and schedule it for six months from now, you may wake up to find that your newsletter auto sent the day after a devastating volcano killed thousands in Indonesia because you forgot what was in it.

2. Your newsletter might be less authentic. It's important that the newsletter reflect you. The you that you are changes over time. Your mood, your interests, your noticings, and even your tone may shift over several months. Energetically speaking, you are more in tune with your readers' questions and concerns at this moment. Your newsletter may be co-created based on questions you're hearing on social media, in your consults, when teaching workshops, etc. These shifts happen subtly over time.

If you're writing about a month ahead, it may work out well for you. The further in advance you're pre-writing, the more concerns you might have.

If you do decide to batch/pre-write your newsletters — especially if they'll go out more than a week after you've written them — *please* **add a note to your calendar to review the message contents the day before the message is scheduled to send.** Add a task on your to-do list, write it in red on your scheduler, set a reminder on your phone, do whatever you have to do to remember that it's going out so that you can check it for relevance and any sensitivity issues prior to sending.

Chapter 12
Editing Your Newsletter

Now that you have a draft to work from, plan to spend *a short amount of time* editing what you've written. You can edit immediately after writing your draft if you like, although I recommend giving yourself at least a few hours and ideally a day or more between writing and editing.

In the last chapter, we defined editing as the process of revising your work for clarity, coherence, and quality so that your message is easily understood by readers. Many people hear "editing" and think immediately of checking for spelling, grammar, and punctuation mistakes. While that is part of the process, it's even more important to review your newsletter to make sure the ideas are expressed clearly and organized well.

I find it helpful to do two rounds of editing: the first to look for conceptual or "big picture" issues and the second to clean up any typos, punctuation errors, and so forth.

Round #1: Check for ideas and flow

When you're writing a book, your manuscript will first undergo something called "developmental editing." Rather than looking for misspelled words and stray commas, a developmental editor reads your draft to make sure it makes sense, looking for places to improve structure, continuity, and organization.

You're going to be your own developmental editor, checking to make sure the ideas and concepts make sense. (Note that if your newsletter is a basic list and/or otherwise doesn't include a written essay, you can skip this stage. If it has any substantial written pieces, though, you'll want to review them at least briefly while you put yourself in the reader's shoes.)

You don't need to spend hours on this. The goal is to do a quick double check with a fresh set of eyes or a new perspective. You've got the ideas on the page, now it's time to organize and evaluate them.

This stage is all about answering one key question: Am I clearly conveying the main point of this newsletter?

Read through your draft and ask yourself what the ONE key takeaway is for the reader. If you aren't sure or if there are several key takeaways, it's time to do some refining.

If there are multiple key takeaways, congratulations! You have written two or more newsletters. This saves you time later. Separate out the two newsletters and pick one to use for now. Focus on the key point you're hoping to make. Is there anything you can do to make this point clearer? Often this will involve either removing unnecessary words/sentences or adding an illustrative story or example.

Group similar ideas together. Update your sentences so that they're clear. Remove unnecessary bits. I often happily repeat myself in the first draft stage, knowing that I'll clean everything up and remove the repetitive bits when I edit.

Limit the time you spend on this. Don't forget, newsletters are typically disposable content. A quick read-through to make sure everything makes sense is fine, especially if you're a more confident writer.

Bring your voice forward when editing

Because this newsletter is part of your business, you may be tempted to think of it as a formal piece of writing. If you had a strict language arts education, you may have been taught to avoid contractions and to use perfectly correct grammar. You'd never dream of starting a sentence with a preposition. The good news is that Mrs. Anderson from sixth grade English isn't here with her red pen.

A newsletter is different from a research paper or an assignment for school.

Here, you want to sound as much like yourself as you can. You do not need to follow APA, MLA, or any other guidelines in your newsletter. Instead, aim for a cadence and tone that help the reader feel like they're hearing you speak.

I recommend using contractions. And, if you want to start a sentence with a preposition, go right ahead. Similarly, if emojis or GIFs fit your style, use them. You want your readers to get a feel for your personality with each newsletter.

If you're having trouble deciding whether your writing sounds like you, try listening instead. Read your newsletter aloud, have a friend read it aloud, or use an automated voice to translate your written words into speech. Does this sound like something you'd say in conversation? If not, how can you edit the language or tone to be more "you"?

If you're a formal person, write a formal newsletter. It'll be right in line with how you show up for clients.

If you're a casual person but you write a formal newsletter, the people who like your newsletter won't be the same ones who like your work. Show up as yourself – the most *you* you can be – in your newsletter. You're enough exactly like you are. You'll likely resonate with readers more if you edit to bring your voice into your newsletter rather than editing yourself out to sound more academic or formal.

Use spacing, headings, bullet points, and bolding to help your readers

As you're revising paragraphs during the first round of editing, remember that most people will be reading on their phones. It's challenging to read large blocks of text on a phone, so ideally, you'll want to have short paragraphs. **I recommend no more than three sentences per paragraph, and it's fine to have a one-sentence paragraph.**

Similarly, particularly if your newsletter is quite long, consider breaking up the text using one or more of the following:

- Add headings to identify key points or themes to facilitate skimming.

- Use lists or bullet points to draw the eye to important information.

- Bold key sentences or phrases so that readers can find them easily.

- Put dividers between sections to make them seem more approachable.

If a quick glance at your newsletter shows a big block of text, readers are more likely to give up or feel intimidated. Break things down so they're easy to read and digest.

Questions for your first round of editing

- Does this piece cover one topic?

- Does it make sense?

- Is the piece useful or relevant to my clients?

- Does the newsletter sound like me?

- If the newsletter is long, have I broken up the text so readers can skim easily?

Round #2: Proofreading

After you feel good about the content and flow of your newsletter, it's time to do one final read-through to catch any lingering "red squiggles" (misspellings, punctuation errors, and so forth). Grammarly can help. Many AI programs will proofread for you as well. Word and Google Docs have built-in grammar, spelling, and punctuation corrections. Everything listed here does need to be double-checked, though, as these programs are not always correct.

Your goal is to do a quick final check for glaring errors. You want to send out something that's professional, but it doesn't need to be perfect.

The exclamation point rule

This is a special rule I've developed for exclamation point lovers. You know who you are. I love you, but it is possible to have too many exclamation points. The occasional exclamation point conveys a friendly and excited tone. Too many exclamation points leave the reader feeling overwhelmed and can come across as disingenuous.

Here's the guideline I recommend: **Allow yourself up to three exclamation points in your newsletter (including the subject line) if your newsletter is three paragraphs or more.** If it's less than three paragraphs, aim for up to two exclamation points. Decide where you want them and delete the rest. Over time, see if you can wean yourself down to just one per newsletter!

Editing goals:

- Punctuation allows your point(s) to be understood

- Short paragraphs make the message easy to read

- Headings, bullet points, bolding emphasize key points

Takeaways and next steps

- When editing a newsletter draft, first check that the concepts and ideas make sense. Aim for one major point per newsletter.

- Your newsletter's tone does not need to be formal. Your voice should shine through.

- Read your newsletter aloud to check that the tone is correct and that the concepts flow nicely.

- Use Grammarly, AI tools, or programs built into your word processing software to help proofread.

- Limit yourself to no more than three exclamation points per newsletter.

Newsletter Tip: Is peer review necessary?

You do not need someone else to look over your newsletter, but if you want feedback, you can send along a draft of your newsletter to a peer, colleague, mentor, or friend. Let them know that you aren't looking for proofreading at this time but that you're interested in their feedback on the concepts.

If this person knows nothing about your field, you may just be looking for very simple info about the ideas you're presenting. Do they understand what you've written? Does it make sense?

If the person has some knowledge of your field, they may be able to provide more specific feedback on the topic: Did I explain this correctly? Is this authentic and true to the values of our field?

However, remember that **you can choose to take or leave any feedback provided by a reviewer.** The pros are that people can catch things you can't see. The cons are that you want the newsletter to be in your voice. You won't always agree with the content suggested by reviewers, and they may have stylistic preferences that don't align with yours.

Many people won't understand your newsletter philosophy and will try to edit to make it more "professional" or to add more information.

Ultimately, it helps to be clear about what specific feedback you're hoping to receive and to remind yourself that you get to decide to keep or leave any suggestions made. If you share a document, I suggest allowing "suggestions" rather than direct edits on your document or sharing a "read-only" version and asking for answers to just a few questions.

Chapter 13

Writing a Clear Subject Line

Your newsletter's subject line will be the first thing your readers see when it's delivered to their inboxes, and it should be the last thing you write when composing your newsletter. Although knowing it's the first thing a reader will see can feel like a lot of pressure, I encourage you to think about your subject line as an extension of your newsletter. Once you know what you're writing about in each newsletter, the subject line will flow naturally from there.

Write your subject line last

After you're finished writing and editing your newsletter, it's time to start formulating your subject line. You might be wondering why we didn't discuss subject lines earlier in this book, when we were creating your newsletter templates. **The reason I recommend writing your subject line last is that the subject line should reflect what is actually in your newsletter.**

Often, what we think we'll write about isn't what comes out when it's time to start writing. Similarly, it's not unusual for a piece to undergo major changes during the first round of editing. It can be hard to know what will wind up in the newsletter until you've finished the first round of editing. Assigning a subject line early in the process can make it harder to change direction later.

Instead, let the subject line be a function of what you write about rather than the other way around.

Write clear subject lines

Although there are people who will try to convince you otherwise, when it comes to your subject lines, **clear is better than clever.**

You don't need to spend loads of time agonizing over the perfect subject line for now. **In the beginning especially, worrying too much about your subject line is more likely to bog you down and prevent you from sending your newsletter than it is to get you a few more opens/clicks/clients.**

You've probably seen articles all about how to write compelling subject lines. You may have even signed up for freebies or read lists of "the 50 best subject lines" from renowned copywriters.

While it is helpful to have a subject line that catches the eye, it's more important to have a consistent subject line that lets your reader know what's in the newsletter. The best way to encourage someone to open your newsletters regularly is to write newsletters they care about and that help them in some way, either by entertaining, encouraging, providing useful information, etc.

This is about the relationship you have with your readers. If you only want them to open an email or two and buy something from you right away, then doing everything you can to get them to open the message becomes especially important. However, if you come from the perspective that the newsletter is about introducing your work to the reader, serving them whether they buy something or not, and letting readers get more comfortable with you and your work to decide whether or not to work with you, then it becomes less critical whether they open any specific newsletter.

Tricks and tactics for better subject lines aren't necessary

The common advice is to have a catchy subject line that readers can't help but open. Even the word *catchy*, as in "I caught you," does not convey the energy we're going for as we build an authentic relationship. The common advice here is to use questions to "leave an open loop" or to work with lists such as, "5 easy ways to..." Do these strategies work to get someone to open your newsletter? Sure, yes.

Most people know on some level that they've just fallen for clickbait when they see a subject line like this. Readers may feel slightly foolish, even as they're opening your message to find out what ONE TRICK you used to have skin as clear and smooth as an undisturbed pond.

If you use a "catchy" subject line, it's imperative that you follow through with whatever you've promised there in the content of your message. The worst case is that your subject line is great, someone clicks through, reads the message, and regrets doing so (or even worse, feels manipulated). What you've done in this case is increased your open rate on this message but decreased it (for this reader at least) on future ones.

Because while readers might open one or two clickbait subject line emails, if the content isn't worth it, they're not going to keep doing that indefinitely.

Instead of getting caught up in finding the perfect subject line, aim for subject lines that are consistent, clearly identify that the message is from you, and clearly identify what the message is about.

Subject line pointers

- Your subject line should feel like you.

- Most email clients will display 40 to 60 characters of the subject line, so keep yours relatively concise.

- Make sure the subject line provides some indication of what's inside the email.

- Use the same format every time.

Subject line examples

For example, my newsletter for practitioners always has a subject line using the following format (no brackets):

- [Topic of main message] + [something from one of my recommendations] [emoji]

Some example subject lines from recent newsletters:

- Periodic business breakdowns + food allergies

- Business slowness + how to be immortal online

- Humanizing emails + summer writing

Other people set apart the newsletter subject line by using the newsletter title in brackets or otherwise emphasized, along with the topic of the newsletter.

For example:

- [Weekly Quick Recipe] Summertime Veggie Soup

- Spring poem and web tip: Issue 338

- **Bloom and Grow Weekly**: Quick hydration tips

You can create subject line consistency with capitalization, punctuation, or the use of emojis:

- ~ dandelions are in bloom ~

- ~ time to harvest your chickweed ~

- Why probiotics might not be the answer to your problems

- Community Healing Events: January 2025

- wintertime recipes and herbal goodies

- Echinacea isn't for everyone

Note that offer emails can have a different style of subject line than your standard newsletter issues. (Offer newsletters are messages entirely devoted to inviting your readers to sign up for one thing. More on these in Chapter 15.)

Activity: Choosing your subject line format

- Look back through subject lines of newsletters you enjoy reading. Are there any themes or examples you could pull from?

- Play around with some different formats. What feels natural, interesting, and right to you?

- Add a reminder about what you've chosen to your writing template.

- Aim for a very similar subject line each week so that your readers can immediately identify your message and know what to expect.

Takeaways and next steps

- Write the subject line last so that it accurately reflects the content of the newsletter after editing.

- Use a consistent format for subject lines to help readers identify your newsletters.

- Identify the topic of your newsletter in the subject line.

- Don't spend too much time creating "catchy" subject lines. Just send the newsletter.

Newsletter Tip: Split testing your subject line isn't necessary

I'm not an advocate for split testing multiple subject lines in the beginning. Once you're regularly writing newsletters and once you have a readership of several hundred people or more, you can start playing around with split testing if you like.

Split testing subject lines is offered by most ESPs, often on the free plans. Split testing means that you come up with two subject lines. The ESP sends out identical versions of your newsletter – other than the subject line – to a small subset of your list (usually 25 percent) and tracks which one gets the most opens over a short period of time (usually a few hours). After that, it selects a winner and uses that subject line to send the message to the other 75 percent of your list.

You can usually adjust these parameters to your taste.

Again, this doesn't make a big difference with a small list, and I'd rather you send your message than worry about this in the beginning.

Eventually, if you like data and playing around with these types of things, go for it. However, you don't need to. You can send out regular newsletters without a ton of data, analytics, or tracking.

Ask yourself what the benefit versus the risk is for this process: Maybe a small increase in percentage of opens, which can add up over time, but is that worth the time, stress, and energy? For some people, it will be; for others, not so much.

Chapter 14

Repurposing Your Newsletters

While sending a high-quality newsletter is a valuable marketing tool and a service to your community, writing regularly has the added benefit of deepening your thoughts and broadening your understanding of the work you do and how it fits into your field.

As you begin writing more regularly, you'll find that writing is a way of understanding and making meaning of your stories and of better understanding what you think, what you have to say, and how you approach your work. We use writing to make meaning, and often ideas emerge as we're writing that we hadn't identified before.

Everyone has access to information. **What makes your newsletter special, intriguing, and useful is how information filters through you – including your experiences (both professional and personal) and how you've made meaning from them.**

Newsletters are co-created

Writing your newsletter is a collaborative process. You're keeping your readers in mind – again, remember that your readers are the people who you'd most like to work with – as you write, and because you are writing and sending regularly, you will start to hear back from people if your work is resonating. Readers will send you ideas, replies, and feedback. You'll also get feedback in the way of data – how many people open, click, and sign up to work with you. (More on this in Chapter 17.)

In this way, you'll begin thinking about your newsletter as something that comes through you but perhaps doesn't entirely belong to you. Your ideas will be shaped by your thoughts and experiences and by the feedback you receive from readers.

It's okay to address topics repeatedly

Many new newsletter writers assume that once you've covered a topic, you can't come back to it. With this perceived pressure to keep thinking up new ideas, it's easy to get stuck or worry that you'll eventually run out of things to write about.

Most readers need to hear concepts repeatedly to truly take them in. We need reminders about things we know but forget to do. It is okay and even ideal to return to key ideas repeatedly. Each time, you'll make your point slightly differently, and each time, you reader may understand it in a new way.

If something resonates with your readers the first time, it will resonate again if you address the same idea later. If you're a nutritionist, for example, you don't just mention that vegetables are good for your client once and assume they'll start eating more broccoli. In fact, clients find it helpful to be reminded of this repeatedly. You can share different tips, tools, ideas, concepts so that each person can find a path forward that works for them, doesn't cause harm, and fits their needs. You could revisit this topic every single week and still have more to say on it.

If you find that you're returning to some topics or themes repeatedly, you have stumbled on what many marketers call "pillar content." You may not know what your pillar content or topics will be until you've been writing for a while. You'll notice that certain ideas come up repeatedly in your writing and work. Things bubble to the surface and your understanding of how they fit into your philosophy will shift a bit as you continue writing, thinking, and discussing.

Never be afraid to revisit these ideas frequently in your newsletter, particularly those that are also resonating with your readers. Each time you share thoughts or reflections on these topics, your work will deepen.

Recycle key content

You might find that some of your newsletters are particularly well-received. If you have a few newsletter issues that you're proud of or that you think are worth revisiting, you can re-send the same newsletter to your list periodically.

Doing this gives you an occasional break from writing and means that people who missed the content the first time because they weren't on your list yet or because they simply overlooked it will have a chance to read it. Readers who saw the message when it was originally sent may appreciate the chance to revisit it.

Some people will post "reruns" when they're on vacation, ill, or even throughout a full season when they want to focus on something else. If you decide to rerun an older piece, you can take the opportunity to refresh the content slightly, you can add a preface noting that this is a rerun, or you can simply send out the message exactly as it went out the first time.

I don't recommend reusing messages until you've been sending newsletters for at least a year. If you're only sending monthly, you might want to wait for two or more years before sending out any repeats.

Activity: Pick a few possible rerun newsletters

Review your old newsletters and pick the best of the bunch based on seasonal/topical relevance, open rates, and/or response rates. You can also select newsletters that hold a special meaning to you or that bear repeating. Keep these issues in a file or folder labeled "Possible Reruns" or something similar. This way, you won't have to search for them again if the need arises.

Put foundational newsletters online

We've talked about how newsletters are disposable content. They tend to come and go easily. There's a certain freedom in this kind of writing since the stakes are low. You can try out material, play with your ideas, and refine your thinking as you revisit topics and gauge the response.

Eventually, you'll write something you'd like to keep or share later.

My general rule of thumb is that **if you or your readers may want to refer to the newsletter content after several months or years, it's best to put it on your website where it'll have a stable link and be more easily accessible as a reference.**

There are a few options for how to handle this:

1. **Post certain newsletter articles on your website as blog posts if they are well-received.** This means you can link to these articles, they are searchable on your website, and they may contribute to your SEO. In this case, you would only post newsletter articles on your website if you felt that this article was pillar content or something that you or a reader might want to return to repeatedly.

2. **Publish all issues of your newsletter on your website as blog posts.** In this scenario, you would include the full article in your newsletter and provide a URL to the post for the reader in case they would like to share or save the article.

3. **Write articles on your website and mention them in your newsletter,** pointing people to your blog if they'd like to read the whole thing. This works well if your piece is particularly long and may feel overwhelming if included in full in a newsletter.

Most of the time, I recommend going with option one. Especially in the beginning, give yourself the space for your newsletters to flow in and out of inboxes without any additional pressure of having them live forever online. Any that wind up being particularly significant, you can choose to post on your website as a blog or an article.

Once you have a larger reader base, deepen your writing voice, and feel more confident that many or most of your newsletters are serving your readers, you might want to transition to option two: posting all newsletter articles publicly online. Some ESPs will offer the option to publish your newsletter online automatically; most do not. This can add a substantial amount of administrative time, so I don't recommend it unless you have good reason to believe that it might be worth the extra time.

(Remember, if you use a writing template outside of your ESP as recommended in Chapter 7, you'll have a copy of each message in case you'd like to reuse them or publish them on your website later.)

Takeaways and next steps

- Writing your newsletter is a way of making meaning from what you experience and your understanding of your work.

- Your newsletter is ultimately co-created with your readers, as you adjust to their interests and what serves them.

- It is okay to revisit key topics or pillar content frequently.

- You can rerun topics or newsletter content during busy seasons.

- Archive valuable content by posting it on your website.

Newsletter Tip: Using AI, templates, or hiring a copywriter

By this point in the book, you may be thinking that newsletter writing seems like quite a bit of work.

Even if you're writing a short newsletter once per month, if you're putting yourself into the process, it takes a great deal of mental and emotional labor.

You may be tempted to turn to ChatGPT or to buy a bundle of email templates or even to hire a copywriter who can write your newsletters for you. You could throw in a few topics, get a draft, make a few tweaks, and get this checked off your list, right?

Although it would be easier to do this, I strongly encourage you to write your newsletters on your own.

If your newsletters are written by AI or by someone else, by definition, they aren't from you. Our intention here is to build relationships between you and your community. When you start with AI or someone else's writing, you're complicating things significantly. We're not trying to send out content for the sake of sending something. We're sharing writing that means something, to allow potential clients to get a feel for who we are, our values, etc.

Using ChatGPT to create a draft newsletter means you're outsourcing your thinking to ChatGPT rather than doing it yourself. The growth and value in shaping your ideas will be diluted in this case.

This is not to say I am against using AI models, copywriters, or email templates in all cases.

Ideas for working with AI in your writing

- **Topic generation:** Have a conversation with an AI model about topics to write about. (Tip: Keep coming back to the same conversation rather than starting a new one each time.)

- **Proofreading:** Ask an AI model if your writing is clear, and have it check for grammar, spelling, and basic edits.

- **Concept review:** Have I left anything out? Does this make sense? Is this true?

- Ask AI to write a draft on the topic after you've written yours, compare the two, and refine based on any new ideas sparked by the AI draft.

Run any feedback through your own filters rather than accepting it without review. For example, AI models will often counsel you to add a call-to-action to your emails, remove language that makes your writing sound like you in favor of more "professional" tone, etc. While those recommendations may make sense in some contexts, for our purposes, they might weaken the email rather than strengthen it.

Using pre-written templates

Many of the same cautions apply to using pre-written newsletter templates. Please don't use them right out of the box, as they won't be "you." However, if you do well with something to start from and you're pretty good at getting your voice and point into the work, you could consider using a template. Just **remember that what comes from within you will be more resonant to your people than something that originates from within someone else.**

Working with a copywriter

Similarly, a good copywriter can meet with you and/or look through your previous writing and emulate your tone well. But good copywriting is expensive. There is value in doing the thinking yourself, in growing as you write, in having a more nuanced understanding of your ideas and where they fit/why they matter that you will miss if you have someone else write for you.

If writing is so hard that you'd rather hire it out (at least at the beginning stages), you might want to consider a different method of staying connected with people who might be interested in your work (see Chapters 16 and 17) or sending a newsletter that relies heavily on video or audio, such as a newsletter that shares recent podcast or YouTube videos.

Chapter 15

Inviting People to Subscribe

Even if your newsletter is perfectly tailored to meet the needs of your readers and to reflect the work you do, in most cases, it won't magically fill your business all by itself. You need to invite people to sign up to receive your newsletter, and you'll periodically want to invite your existing readers to work with you.

Your newsletter's role in marketing

Marketing your work is a multi-step process. Your newsletter will work for several of these steps, but not all of them. Often, beginners are under the impression that by starting a newsletter, you'll automagically draw in readers. The right people will flock to your website, and your subscription numbers will quickly grow. **A newsletter is only one piece of a full marketing plan.** If you're expecting to write a newsletter, do no other marketing, and grow your practice, you're bound to be disappointed.

Your newsletter only works to bring in more 1:1 clients if people know about it and sign up to receive it. Furthermore, the people who sign up and read the newsletter are ideally people who you'd like to work with and who you could reasonably expect to help. (See Chapter 4.) You're looking for "good fit" readers and not just warm bodies to add to the list.

For your newsletter to effectively be part of your marketing plan, here's what needs to be in place:

    1. You meet people who do not already know about you and your

work and who are potentially the types of clients with whom you'd like to work.

2. You invite these new people to join your newsletter.

3. There is a compelling reason for these people to sign up for your newsletter.

4. You send your newsletter regularly.

5. Your newsletter resonates with your readers, provides value, and reflects your work and perspective.

6. You periodically invite people to work with you 1:1 in your newsletter.

Tell people your newsletter exists

Once again, simply having a newsletter does not mean people will subscribe to it. **Your newsletter is not a way to meet people who don't already know about you** – particularly in the beginning.

Once you've been sending it for a while and once you have a newsletter that resonates with your readers, you might get some new folks joining your newsletter because it was forwarded to them by someone else. This is rare, however.

Let's assume you're not quite there yet.

In addition to writing your newsletter (and sending it), you need ways to meet people who don't already know about you and your work. These can include:

• Teaching classes or workshops online

• Teaching classes or workshops in person

- Building a referral network

- Being a guest on someone else's podcast or blog

- Advertising

- SEO

- Talking about your work in your daily life

When you meet people who might be a good fit for the work you do in one of these contexts, you'll want to explicitly mention your newsletter and invite them to sign up.

Here are ways to do this:

- During the registration process for a class, workshop, or any other type of gathering, ask if the registrant would like to sign up for your newsletter to find out about future events.

- At the end of a class or workshop, explain a bit about your newsletter, what you send out/why someone would want to subscribe, and pass around a list for people to sign up.

- After an event, send a follow-up email with relevant references, links, or resources. In this email, write a concise description of what your newsletter offers and include an invitation to subscribe.

- During an event, mention that your next newsletter will include [topic relevant to people at the event] and share how people can sign up to receive it if they'd like.

- During an in-person event, have a clipboard, QR code, or other way for attendees to sign up to join your newsletter. Again, make it clear why they might want to subscribe.

- Add a succinct description of your newsletter and a link to subscribe in the signature of your professional email.

- Send peers, colleagues, former teachers, etc. a brief note letting them know that you're starting (or revamping!) your newsletter, who it's for, and why someone might want to sign up, and provide a link to pass along in case they know of anyone who might be interested.

Activity: Plan activities to get new subscribers

Pick one or two activities you can do to meet people who do not already know about your work. Create a specific plan for how often you will do these activities and how you will invite people to sign up for your newsletter over the next three to six months.

What I will do to meet people who don't yet know about my work:

- Include as many specifics as possible. For example, *I will teach one workshop each month.*

How I will invite these people to subscribe to my newsletter:

- Again, be as specific as possible. *I will ask each person if they would like to join my newsletter when they register for the workshop. Here's the text I will use: "[your name] writes a [weekly] newsletter for [people] that [what your newsletter offers]. If you'd like to sign up, [click here, add your name here, reply, etc.]."*

Have a compelling reason to subscribe

To keep yourself focused, it's valuable to think through the implied or explicit promise you are making to newsletter readers. What are you hoping your readers will get from receiving your newsletter? Why would someone want to receive it? We know that your intention is to bring in more 1:1 clients and to serve your community. The service part is what makes it worthwhile for someone to continue receiving and reading your newsletter.

In short: Why would your potential clients want to subscribe?

If you can answer this question succinctly and keep your answer in mind each time you're writing a newsletter, you'll be in excellent shape.

The reasons someone might subscribe include:

1. You're offering a free thing or a discount. (This isn't necessarily the best option, for reasons we'll get into later.)

2. They want to know about your upcoming classes and offerings (or blog posts or...). In this case, they want to receive an informational newsletter.

3. The content of the newsletter is helpful in some way: Perhaps it includes a weekly recipe or a tip about something that matters to them.

4. Your messages feel good to receive – they're encouraging or uplifting or funny, etc.

Why you don't need a "lead magnet"

Almost everyone who teaches about newsletters proposes that the very best way to get people to sign up for your newsletter is to offer a compelling "lead magnet" or a "freebie" – essentially, you provide something of value in exchange for an email address. The idea is that this free thing should be something your clients want that directly reflects the work you do, giving them a chance to sample your work and (hopefully) be impressed with your knowledge, skill, and/or personality.

I don't think you need one. In fact, I think having a freebie may wind up being a detriment overall.

First, let me say that a freebie will likely cause your newsletter subscriber number to grow more quickly than it would without a freebie. (Although this is not always true.)

However, think carefully about if you want or need a freebie before you spend time and energy making one.

Pros

- Readers get to sample your work.

- You can help people right from their first interaction with you.

- They are more likely to open your first email if there is a gift/freebie inside.

- Your list may grow faster than it would otherwise.

Cons

- People may subscribe only because they want the thing and not your newsletters. (They are "settling" for your newsletters but feel manipulated into getting it when all they wanted was the free thing.)

- It takes time and energy to create a freebie, and many of them don't send the message you're hoping they'll send.

- The people who sign up are interested in free things. Often, these are not the kinds of people who want to pay for services as they prefer a DIY approach.

- If something goes wrong with your freebie (automation is weird, links are broken), someone's first experience with you may be a frustrating one.

- If your subscribers live in places with strong consumer protection laws (for example, the EU), you will need to ensure that they are actively consenting to receiving your freebie and to subscribing to your mailing list, which typically involves adding a checkbox for each of these to your sign-up form. There should be the option to only receive the freebie and not subscribe to your mailing list, which adds some extra tech adventure to your setup.

So, if you do decide to do a freebie:

- Make sure it is reflective of the type of work you do – demonstrating your skill, knowledge, and the energy/personality of your practice. It should feel personal and reflect your work.

- Make sure it is something that the clients you want to work with are interested in. Does it somehow relate, very specifically, to this population?

- Triple check that it is set up properly, that it is delivered immediately, and that when it is delivered, it looks professional and is in a usable format. If needed, make sure subscribers are explicitly opting into both the freebie and your newsletter.

- Create a note for yourself to evaluate your free offer(s) at least once per year to determine if they are still valid, current, and reasonable for the types of clients with whom you're hoping to work. Can you improve upon them?

- Remember that more is not better. Some freebies are so large/overwhelming as to be unusable by most readers.

- The freebie should align with the topic of your newsletter. People who want this freebie could reasonably be anticipated to have interest in what you are sending out weekly, monthly, etc.

My experience removing lead magnets from my website

I used to believe that a freebie was mandatory. Over the years, I developed several freebies that did seem to serve me well. When I was working in the fertility/pregnancy space, I had a list of herbs I considered safe in pregnancy and lactation that I used as a freebie. When my business shifted toward mentoring other practitioners, I offered a business-starting checklist as a freebie and a webinar on how to find clients without social media, among other things.

What happened over time is that:

1. It became challenging to maintain all these freebies. If something needed to be changed with my ESP or the integration between my website and the software, I had to track down each instance and update it. I needed to look at each automation periodically to make sure they were working and that the copy was still correct. It felt like a lot, particularly for someone running a one-woman business who had plenty of better things to do.

2. I began to feel increasingly uncomfortable with the idea that I was manipulating people into signing up for my list.

Eventually, in a fit of inspiration – and in a fit of procrastinating on another task – I decided to do away with freebies altogether. Now, if you want to sign up for my mailing list, there is simply an invitation to subscribe with a description of why you'd want to.

I didn't get rid of my freebies. In fact, now I have them all on a single page of my website, where anyone can access them without providing an email address. For convenience, I do offer to email the freebies to anyone who asks, with the option to join my mailing list or not. As of 2024, after several years of having this offer, only five people have ever asked me to email them the freebies without joining my mailing list. Everyone else has opted to join the list.

I suspected that my new subscriber rate would decrease after I made this change. I'd always been told that the freebies were the main thing attracting people to your mailing list. However, I didn't find that to be the case at all. (Note that not all variables were the same during this time, and it's true that I perhaps could have had even MORE new subscribers had I kept the free offers up.) What I did find is that people continue to join my newsletter at a steady pace and that those who join typically want to be there. My unsubscribe rate remains at about 0.2 percent per month or less. To me, this is a win-win situation. **I don't have to maintain a bunch of freebies, and I feel comfortable knowing that everyone on my list has chosen to be there because they want to receive newsletters from me.**

Activity: Update your newsletter subscribe form

Review the sections you chose to include in Chapter 6 and the adjectives you chose to describe your work in Chapter 5. Then, craft a description of why someone might subscribe by completing the activity below:

- You might want to subscribe to my newsletter if:

- Each [week/month/etc.], you'll receive:

- My newsletter provides unique insights on _____ that you won't find anywhere else.

- I started this newsletter because _____, and I want to share that with you through _____.

Now, take this information and update the newsletter sign-up form on your website:

- Subscribe to receive [weekly] [what you send in your newsletter]

- Sign up for [what your newsletter is about] each [timing]

- Get [xxx] in your inbox every [timing]

Example

My website sign-up form says:

Sign up for weekly Practitioner Notes from Camille.
Tips, resources, & encouragement for herbalists & nutritionists, delivered to your inbox most Thursdays

Welcome email sequences: yes or no?

Once someone joins your newsletter, you have a few options:

1. Send one automated welcome email and add them to your main mailing list.

2. Send several automated welcome emails before adding them to your main mailing list.

3. Add the new subscriber to your regular list so they receive the next newsletter scheduled to go out without receiving any welcome email.

4. Send a personal welcome email individually while also sending the next regularly scheduled newsletter.

There are more complicated options, but for our purposes, you'll pick from these four.

If you've promised a freebie, you'll pick either number one or number two.

If you're overwhelmed and not techie, my recommendation is to start with number three or number four.

Choices #1 and 2: Sending automated welcome emails

If you like or at least tolerate tech setup and have the bandwidth to draft a welcome email or sequence, do that. It's the "optimized" thing to do.

First, you'll want to set up an automation in your ESP. This varies depending on which ESP you're using. You can look up how to do it or contact their tech support.

First email: Say hello, send the freebie if you've promised one, ask if they have any questions, or share a bit about yourself.

Additional emails: The idea with an automation sequence is to send a few "welcome" emails to help the new subscriber get a better feel for who you are, your work, and what you have to offer. Typically, these are spaced with three to seven days between each one. Here are some things you could do in your welcome emails:

- Share three to five pieces of your best or most popular content.

- Invite someone to join you on social media or to subscribe to your podcast.

- Share a bit about what you do and invite them to sign up to work together.

There isn't a single correct way to do these things, so just imagine what you'd want to send out if one of your best friends signed up and didn't already know much about what you've been up to in your professional life. What are the highlights?

If you're sending an automation sequence and not just a single welcome email, I recommend not adding someone to your main mailing list until after they've worked through your welcome

sequence. Otherwise, they may get multiple emails from you on a single day or in a single week.

These welcome emails should use the same salutation, sign-off, bio, and formatting (fonts, heading style, logo placement, etc.) you use in your regular newsletters.

Remember, though, when you're building a relationship with your new readers, you don't need to convince them to buy anything right away. They don't need to enter a funnel or cross a tripwire. **Your goal is to share a bit about yourself and your work so the new reader is oriented and has a chance to see your best stuff that they may not have seen since they've just met you and come across your work.**

Choice #3: Add new subscribers directly to your regular list

Technically, that first email you send to new subscribers is an important one and the one they're most likely to open. However, if the idea of setting up an automation and creating one or more welcome emails is overwhelming, it's more important to allow people to join your list so they can receive your regular newsletter.

Give yourself time to adjust to that before stressing out too much about a welcome email. For the first five years (!) I ran my practitioner newsletter, I never quite got around to creating a welcome email. People signed up on my website and then received their first message from me when my regular newsletter went out each Thursday. My newsletter grew my business consistently during this time.

If this is what you have the bandwidth for, it's not a problem. Start here and add automations or welcome emails later as your capacity increases or when the mood strikes.

Choice #4: Send a personal welcome email

I learned this technique from business coach Jenny Shih, who pointed out that if you have a small list, it's reasonable to send a personal email to each new subscriber welcoming them and asking if they have any questions. As your list grows, this may not be feasible, but in the beginning, doing this can build relationships with new people and feel quite welcoming.

Here's an example email that you could send when you notice a new subscriber coming through:

Hi [name],

I saw that you signed up for my newsletter recently. Thanks so much for being here!

I like to touch base with new subscribers just to say hello and to find out if you have any questions about [whatever you do]. I love hearing from people, so please reply here or to any of my regular newsletters if I can help you with anything.

[your signature],

[Your Name]

P.S. This is not an automated email – it really is just me, writing to you.

Note that these can be sent at any point – a day after the person subscribes, a week later, or even several weeks or a month later.

Send these emails individually, from your business email account (not through your ESP). If people reply with questions, these can make great fodder for future newsletters or other content, and if nothing else, your exchange may open new doors down the line. Do not directly promote anything in a personal email sent from your regular email account, as you may run afoul of data processing laws if you do this.

Activity: Create your welcome email or sequence

Decide how you will welcome new subscribers to your newsletter. Set up automation sequences if needed. Draft a personalized message if you're choosing option four. Whether you're doing anything special to welcome new subscribers or not, this is a good time to double check that all subscribe forms on your website, social media, etc. are working properly.

Takeaways and next steps

- For your newsletter to bring in more 1:1 clients, you must meet new people and invite them to sign up for your newsletter.

- Your newsletter sign-up form should explain why someone would want to sign up.

- Once someone has joined, you can welcome them by sending a freebie, by sending a private message, by sending automated messages, or by simply adding them to your list.

- Create a plan for how you will meet people who do not yet know about your business and how you will invite these people to subscribe to your newsletter.

- Update your newsletter sign-up form to share what readers will receive/why they would want to subscribe.

- Test the subscription process to make sure new subscribers are being added to the correct list and that any automation or welcome emails are being delivered.

Newsletter Tip: Technology woes

If you're pulling your hair out trying to get a technical situation sorted out when it comes to your newsletter, here is my advice.

First: Are you making this harder than it needs to be? You don't need fancy automations. You don't need a branded template. You don't need images in your newsletters. Can you simply draft a normal email in a document and paste it into a blank email within your ESP? If so, do that and click send.

Second: If you're having a tech issue getting set up or changing to a new platform – especially one-time situations like getting your domain authenticated or connecting your website and your newsletter subscribe form – just go ahead and hire someone to help you.

What will take you four hours will often take someone who knows what they're doing four minutes. Try Upwork or ask friends and colleagues for a referral. There is someone for almost any tech woe on Upwork.

The most important things about your newsletter are that it sounds like you and that you send it regularly. The more it looks like a regular email that you'd send to a colleague rather than a promotion for a Labor Day clothing sale, the better.

Keep it simple and skip the tech stress if you can.

Chapter 16

Inviting Readers to Work with You

Once someone is subscribed to your newsletter, you now can share more about what you do, be of service, and periodically invite them to work with you 1:1.

It's easy to think that by promoting yourself, you're bothering people or "cluttering up" their inboxes. **People who like your work will want to know when you have something to offer.** They are predisposed to being interested in what you're doing. If your offer isn't for them, they will delete or ignore the message and move on.

The keys to effective promotional newsletters are to:

1. Send them infrequently.

2. Write them in your own voice.

3. Send a heartfelt invitation rather than a pressure-filled pitch.

4. Highlight the change or results you hope clients will receive.

Much of the work that's needed for a reader to become a 1:1 client is done before you send the offer letter: helping the client understand what you do and how you approach your work and feeling comfortable that the two of you are a good fit to work together. The offer email is simply an explicit invitation for them to sign up if the time is right.

Don't over-offer your services

Some newsletter courses and experts will recommend that you have a single clear call-to-action in every newsletter. Calls-to-action can include asking the reader to reply to the message, asking them to sign up for an offer or waitlist, or asking them to click on a specific link.

While this may make sense for some types of newsletters, for our purposes, doing this may not be the best idea.

Why?

1. Every single newsletter winds up feeling transactional or manipulative to the reader. Yes, there may be valuable information in the message, and most people don't take kindly to being asked for something – especially money – every time you interact.

2. After a while, readers who are finding value in your work will eventually tune out your invitations (calls-to-action) if they are present in every message.

3. The invitations are lost among the other content in your message. Providing value and weaving in a call-to-action means that the invitation may be overlooked if the person doesn't read all the way through carefully.

Defining 'offer' newsletters

An offer or promotional newsletter is an entire issue devoted exclusively to letting readers know about your offer, how to tell if they're a good fit, and information about how to get started. You can send an offer newsletter instead of or in addition to your regular newsletter. The offer letter does not include any of your regular newsletter sections (other than your bio).

Your bio, which is included in each newsletter, will have information about how to work with you and what you do, but many people won't read to the very end of your newsletters. (Refer to Chapter 8 for suggestions on writing your bio.)

Similarly, creating content that relates to a service you offer and mentioning at the end of the piece or in a P.S. at the bottom that readers can work with you 1:1 if they need help is also not counted as an offer for our purposes, although it can be effective in some cases!

Send offer newsletters 20-25% of the time

I wish I could tell you the exact amount of offer newsletters that will work for you and your practice. The answer varies depending on your situation. **A good rule of thumb is to make an offer every four to five emails.** So, if you're sending a weekly newsletter, aim to send a specific offer newsletter about once per month. If you're sending seasonally, you may send out an offer newsletter just two or three times per year. Again, these **offer newsletters can be sent in addition to or instead of your regularly scheduled newsletters.**

Some people never send out an email dedicated only to making an offer and instead prefer to put all upcoming services, classes, and offers in an "Upcoming Events" section of their normal newsletter. If that works for you and if people are signing up for your offers, that may be all you need.

It's been my experience, however, that **unless you send at least one dedicated email invitation, many people will overlook or forget about your offer.** For example, if I have an upcoming class that has been mentioned in three or even four regular newsletters and then send out a dedicated offer email the day of the class, somewhere between 75 and 90 percent of the people who attend will sign up from the offer newsletter.

I typically send an offer newsletter about once per month. I usually send offer newsletters on a Monday, and they are sent in addition to my regular newsletter, which goes out each Thursday.

Offers remind readers of your work

Not long after I began offering courses and programs for practitioners, I created a course on how to find more 1:1 clients. I was still leery of overselling in my newsletter and felt hesitant to bother anyone. I mentioned the course two or three times in my regular newsletter (which was going out every other week at that time) and sent one "invitation-focused" newsletter about the course to my whole list as well.

A few weeks after the course started, I heard from one newsletter reader who was disappointed because she hadn't realized the class was happening and would have signed up if she'd known. This was just the type of person I most wanted to work with and someone who most likely reads my newsletter more closely than most people.

Even she hadn't known about the course after multiple mentions and one devoted message.

What I took away from this – and I've learned the same lesson from being a university professor for more than 15 years – is that even people who love your work and who want to sign up for your services/offerings may need repeated reminders. **Letting people know what services are available to them is a service.**

You may feel like you're bothering your readers, but remember that only a fraction of subscribers will open any given email, and of those that open, many will get distracted as they're reading. Reminders are helpful and welcomed by folks who do want to work with you.

Be specific about how you can help

It is much easier to say "yes" to a clear invitation when you know exactly what is being offered, who is a good fit, and how to sign up.

For example, if you're inviting a friend who lives in another state to visit your house for the weekend, you could say, "Come by anytime. I'd love to see you." Or you could say, "I'm around the last weekend in March, we have a guest room, and there's a great new restaurant in town I think you'd love. Does it work in your schedule to visit that weekend?"

These are both invitations, but one is much easier to accept.

When you're writing an offer for your 1:1 service, you don't need to get weirdly manipulative or use special sales language. You don't need a countdown timer or seventeen "buy now" buttons or extra exclamation points.

All you need to do is cover the following, in your own words:

- What problem or issue you help people with

- What it's like to have this problem and/or who you help

- How you help, including what people changes/results people can expect when they're done working with you

- What's involved in your offer

- How to sign up or learn more

Work from this place: "I have an offer that I think could really help if you're in [this] situation. You may want to sign up so that [what the result is]. I have openings [this month] if you feel ready to start. Here's what's involved, and here's how to sign up."

I'm not providing a template here because **these messages work best if you write them in your own words, from the heart.** Imagine you're sitting in front of someone who's asked for your help. You want to explain to this person a bit about what you do, who it's for, and how it would work if they signed up. You can even say that we could start tomorrow or next week or that you have an opening on Tuesday. And then, you leave it up to them whether it's a good fit or not.

Here's a phrase you can borrow in these messages if you like: "I have [several, two] openings for new clients in [month/season/week]." This gives people a sense of time and availability, without providing undue pressure or falsely claiming that you only have one spot open when in fact you're wide open as far as the eye can see.

Remember, an invitation is just that: an opportunity for someone to say "yes" or "no." Both are acceptable answers. You are not coercing someone into being your client. You're letting them know more about what's involved and providing a specific invitation to join you.

As a reminder, don't slide in extra content. This email is only about your offer. Put anything else you want to mention in your next regular newsletter.

Send reminder emails if your offer has a deadline

If there is a deadline associated with your offer, you may want to send several reminders as the deadline approaches. For example, if there is a price increase, a limited number of spots, a registration deadline, or a special price happening, you can mention this in your messages.

A reasonable cadence in this case is to send one dedicated sales message with all the information someone might need about the offer and how to sign up a week or more before the deadline. You can then send two or even three reminders as the deadline approaches. Reminder emails don't necessarily need to repeat information, although you can provide additional content (reviews, case studies, stories, or FAQs). Will some people unsubscribe when you send offer emails or multiple reminders? Yes. Yes, they will.

Folks who are bothered by receiving a few extra messages from you are not people who were ever going to work with you 1:1 in the first place. It's perfectly okay for those folks to leave your list. Most people will simply ignore or delete messages that don't apply to them, and some may find it quite helpful to receive reminders about something they were hoping to sign up for.

Making offers for small programs or events

You may have multiple smaller programs or offers throughout the year. For example, you may have a monthly or seasonal herb walk or cooking class or you may periodically offer a workshop at the local community college or library. Whether these are free or paid, you might not have enough newsletter "real estate" to send a separate invitation for each of these, particularly if you have a monthly or seasonal newsletter.

If you consistently offer these types of programs, I recommend adding an "Upcoming Events" category to your newsletter template. You can invite people to these programs in this section without needing to send a separate email for each one. Do experiment with sending separate sales emails for each one! You'll find what feels right to you and what works for your situation. **You always have the option to send the solo offer newsletter for larger events, those upon which your income relies, or if you simply feel like it.**

Experiment with your own pacing

As with everything in this book, you may need to adjust these guidelines based on your readers, your business, and your preferences. If sending an offer newsletter every four to five messages doesn't feel right to you, experiment by making an offer in every newsletter, alternate offer messages and regular newsletters, or make offers less frequently. Different strategies work for different people.

Notes about formatting for your offer newsletters

Keep your formatting consistent with your regular newsletters when you send offer newsletters. While you won't be using the same sections in an offer newsletter, you'll still want to include the same fonts, colors, logo placement, greeting, sign-off, and bio. This provides consistency and reminds your readers of previous messages they've found beneficial.

Activity: Draft an offer newsletter

Write down how often you plan to make an offer on your Newsletter Framework Worksheet. If you have multiple offers to promote, decide which ones you'll promote over the next two to three months.

Next, start drafting your offer newsletter. While I don't necessarily recommend having peers look over regular newsletters each time, offer newsletters are an exception. It can be quite helpful to run your offer newsletter by a colleague, peer, or friend to get feedback on the tone, clarity, and copy.

Save your offer newsletters in your writing software so that you can reuse or build upon them the next time you make a similar offer.

Takeaways and next steps

- Your readers want to know when you have something to offer them; don't be scared to let them know!

- Plan to periodically send offer or sales emails that only contain information about an upcoming program or service with a link to sign up.

- Send one offer or invitation email for every four to five standard newsletters. Adjust the cadence for your own business after observing what works.

- Keep your formatting (fonts, logo, colors, etc.) the same for offer emails.

Newsletter Tip: How a newsletter can replace social media

If you'd rather not be on social media, if you're looking to cut back on social media, or if you've tried social media and it's not working very well to bring you 1:1 clients, a newsletter can be an alternative. (It can also be a supplement; you don't have to choose one or the other.)

Both social media and newsletters offer a way for potential clients to get to know you and for you to make periodic invitations to join your 1:1 services or programs.

It is entirely possible to avoid or cut back on social media if you regularly send a newsletter that is helpful or interesting to the people with whom you want to work and if the newsletter feels like an expression of your work.

I left social media in 2018 as I was noticing how much of an effect it had on my mental health. I meant to take a break for a few months until after the midterm elections in the US, but it wound up being so nice that I simply never went back.

At the time, I had built up a relatively large follower count on Facebook (many more people were following me there than were subscribed to my newsletter) and it felt a bit risky to leave all of that behind. I wasn't sure if my business would be okay without social media, but in fact, I've been able to keep my business running and growing steadily without social media and without paid advertising because of my newsletter.

Most people sound more like themselves on social media because they understand that it's an informal/casual environment, so there's less pressure to be perfect or "professional."

The trick is to keep this same mindset when writing your newsletters and to show up regularly by sending newsletters that make a difference.

Chapter 17

How to Tell If Your Newsletter Is Working

Newsletter effectiveness tends to grow over time. At first, it can seem like it's not working at all to bring in more clients. You're writing and sending and nothing is happening. No new clients. No responses. Just...nothing.

This can be quite demoralizing.

A newsletter has what I like to call long legs. Your writing today may not have an immediately noticeable impact, but it becomes more effective over time.

This is exactly what I tell clients about herbal infusions. Some herbs help acutely, but it's more common not to notice any difference whatsoever after taking an herbal tea once. Even after a week, you may not notice much.

However, after drinking an herbal tea daily for a few weeks or a few months, the effects can be profound.

It's about having the patience to wait for the effects to kick in.

Your newsletter – and in fact, many marketing practices – are like this. You may need to keep writing regularly for months (or even years if your newsletter only comes out seasonally or monthly) to notice a difference.

Each issue may touch someone – multiple someones – but the newsletter's cumulative effects grow each time you send one. Readers will see your name repeatedly. They'll get to know your personality. They begin feel connected and to get a sense for who you are and the work you do. You become woven together in an ecosystem of sorts.

This all takes time.

After many months or years, you'll find that the newsletter momentum builds on itself. But you need the patience to keep going and to understand that this is a long-term process, not a "fix it now," one-time action.

How do you know you're moving in the right direction? There are small signs along the way to keep an eye on without getting bogged down in analytics and data.

Your subscriber count doesn't matter (much)

As author and podcaster Jay Acunzo says, resonance is more important than reach.

It doesn't matter how many people subscribe to your newsletter if hardly any of them are people who want to work with you. A smaller number of people who appreciate your approach is much more helpful than thousands of people who tolerate you or who can't recall why they signed up in the first place.

Here are the key things I look for in the first few years that suggest your newsletter is on the right track:

- Your subscriber count is slowly but surely increasing each month.

- A substantial number of your subscribers are opening and reading your messages.

- The people who join seem to be the kind of people with whom you'd enjoy working.

That's it.

If these things are happening, don't worry about the absolute numbers.

If they aren't happening, then look at your marketing plan (are you inviting people to join; do they know about your newsletter?) and how you're describing your newsletter to make sure it's appealing to the type of clients with whom you want to work. (Is this something they need or want? If not, it may be time to reconsider your format or how you're describing what you do.)

The checklist later in this chapter will help you troubleshoot if you think things may be off track.

How many subscribers do I need?

Not very many.

You'll see courses, programs, and services that teach you how to get your first thousand, ten thousand, or more subscribers.

To build a 1:1 practice, you don't need to have a massive audience.

It's not about getting "people" to sign up for your email list. It's about inviting the right people – folks who could use what you offer and with whom you'd like to work – to join you. **A small list full of people who love your work and support what you're doing will be much more likely to support your business than a large list full of people who hardly ever read what you write or who have no interest in paying money for the types of services you offer.**

Sometimes I hear people say, "I only have 12 (or 50 or 150) subscribers." It's tempting to think your newsletter doesn't matter very much when you "only" have a handful of folks subscribed.

However, if you were teaching a class for twelve people, would that be a disappointment? Most of us would be delighted to teach a class with twelve interested folks in attendance. We'd want it to be an excellent experience for these twelve humans. These are real people who are interested in what you have to say.

Don't worry about the fact that someone else has a thousand or ten thousand subscribers. You don't need that many. Keep your eyes on your own page, and show up for the people who are waiting to hear from you.

For 1:1 work, particularly 1:1 work that involves ongoing relationship, you do not need a huge list. The general rule of thumb is that about 1 to 2 percent of people will buy any specific offer from a mailing list. This means if you have one hundred subscribers, one to two will sign up for something when you make an offer. However, I've found that when your list of people is aligned well and full of the right people, this number can be substantially higher.

What you can learn from analytics

When you send out an email newsletter, there's a lot more tracking happening than many people realize. While it's not as invasive as the data collection on social media, it can still surprise those who are new to the world of newsletters.

The basics of newsletter analytics

One of the primary services you get from most ESPs, whether you are on a free or paid plan, is analytics. These analytics typically include the open rate, which tells you how many people opened your email. Analytics can also show you how many people clicked on each link, as well as who clicked on each one, when, and how many times.

I remember feeling surprised and a bit creeped out when I first learned about the extent of this tracking. Knowing that I can see such specific information about readers feels invasive. I think of my email subscribers as colleagues, and I don't like the idea of tracking or spying on them – even if that's not exactly what it is.

Addressing privacy concerns

This topic came up recently when someone who had just started her practice reached out to me. She didn't want to be on social media and had decided to use an email newsletter instead. After sending out a few newsletters, she found the tracking aspect unsettling.

Here are some steps that might help if you share these concerns:

Consider your service provider: Depending on which ESP you use, you might be able to turn off some tracking features. Most ESPs will still track open rates, but some, like Buttondown and MailerLite, offer options to disable certain tracking elements. However, these privacy-focused services may come with trade-offs, like limited segmentation capabilities, or require more tech-savvy to set up.

Focus on top-level analytics: Instead of diving into detailed data on individual subscribers, look at overall statistics. Metrics like open rates and click rates (e.g., 20 percent open rate and 2 percent click rate) can provide valuable feedback on what's working for your readers without feeling invasive. I usually wait 24 hours after sending an email before checking these stats to give a more accurate reflection of engagement.

Look for patterns: Over time, analytics can reveal patterns in subscriber behavior. For example, certain topics might consistently get higher engagement, while others might lead to unsubscribes. This doesn't necessarily mean you should change your content – sometimes it just helps you understand your audience better.

Respect privacy: Personally, I avoid looking at data that tracks specific individuals' actions. While this information is available through most ESPs, I find it invasive and prefer not to use it.

Data is not always accurate

The open rates reported by your ESP may not be perfectly accurate. Many email services and privacy tools block some tracking features and thus do not report when emails are seen or opened. This limitation means the numbers aren't perfect, but they can still provide useful insights.

What to track and how often

While understanding if your newsletter is working is important, you don't want to get too caught up in the numbers. The goal is to connect with real people, and it may take some time for you to find your stride.

After you've set up your plan for finding new subscribers, I recommend following that plan and **consistently writing your newsletter for six to twelve months before making any decisions about whether or not this strategy is working.**

Review your newsletter stats monthly

At the end of each month, spend some time assessing your business progress overall. I allot 20 to 30 minutes at the beginning of each month to gather my numbers for the previous month. I record things like income, expenses, and other numbers that matter to my business.

Relating to newsletters, I suggest tracking the following at the end of each month:

- Your plan for meeting new people (e.g., total number of webinars and attendance at each)

- Total subscribers

- New subscribers

- Newsletters sent out

- For each newsletter: open rate, click-through rate, and number of replies

- Notes about each newsletter (did it spur other topic ideas, how you felt about what you wrote, links that were popular, flag for repurposing or resending later)

Carve out time for seasonal planning and tracking

At the end of each season, it's time to do bigger-picture review and planning. I set aside time each season to think about a goal or intention for the upcoming season, as well as to review progress over the past season.

When it comes to your newsletter, you can use this time to review your overall marketing plan, to set goals for how you'll connect with new people, how many new subscribers you'd like to see, how many newsletters you plan to send, and which offers you'll make during the upcoming season.

This is a chance to adjust your plan based on what did or did not work in the previous season. You can assess this more clearly if you've been doing your monthly tracking! You can also use this time to reach out for help from a mentor, colleague, or teacher if you find that you aren't on track and you aren't sure what to do next.

Again, you can use or modify my seasonal and monthly planning document to set your goals for the upcoming season or to assess your progress. This document is available on the book resources page https://writebetterletters.com/resources. I also host free planning workshops as the start of each season approaches. The link for the planning workshops is also available on the book resources page.

Activity: Schedule time for monthly and seasonal planning

Open your calendar and pick a time at the end of each month (or at the beginning of the following month) to go through your numbers. Schedule in about 30 minutes to do this. If you put the time in your planner now for the next two to three months, it will be easier to remember.

Next, schedule in time for seasonal assessment and planning at the beginning of each upcoming season. I try to do these in mid-December, mid-March, mid-June, and mid-September (around the time of equinox and solstice), although you could also plan yours around the traditional business quarters.

I've included a copy of my seasonal and monthly planning document for you to use or modify on the book resources page.

Newsletter effectiveness checklist

If your newsletter isn't growing or if it isn't turning into new clients, you'll want to figure out what's going on and how to improve. **Remember, no one writes a perfect newsletter immediately. You'll likely need to observe and adjust factors in each of these categories over months or years to create something that works for you, your readers, and your practice.**

Here's a checklist of things to consider.

New subscribers

If you don't have a plan in place for meeting new folks and/or if you meet new people but don't tell them about your newsletter, your newsletter is unlikely to grow. If you didn't have as many new subscribers as you'd hoped, answer the following questions:

- **Did you meet new people this month?** If not, plan to get in front of new people in the months ahead.

- **Did you invite those people to join your newsletter?** Did you clearly ask them to sign up, tell them how to do so, and provide a good reason to do so? If not, plan how you can improve here going forward.

- **Is your newsletter subscribe form working properly?** Check any website subscribe forms, links in your social media bios, email signature, and other places to make sure they are working.

- **Does your newsletter subscribe form describe why someone would want to sign up?** Read this over yourself and/or have a colleague or friend have a look as well. Consider adjusting the language.

- **Is this reason compelling to the types of people you want to work with?** Again, ask a friend or colleague to brainstorm if needed.

Sending your newsletter

If you have plenty of people signing up for your list but you send messages infrequently or messages that aren't reflective of your readers' interests and your own approach, people are unlikely to sign up for 1:1 work.

- **Did you send your newsletter regularly?** How many did you send compared to how many you planned? Can you make more time in your schedule to send regularly?

- **Was your newsletter content useful to your readers?** If people are subscribed but rarely opening or clicking your messages, you might need to rethink the format or content of your newsletters.

- **Does your newsletter sound and feel like you?**

Making offers and sharing what you do

Someone can regularly read your newsletter and not have a clue that you offer 1:1 client support if you never mention your services. If you rarely share what you do and why someone might want to sign up, those people are unlikely to become clients.

- **Do you have a bio in your newsletter that mentions what you do and how to book an appointment?** If not, add one. Consider changing the wording a bit if you aren't in love with what you have now.

- **Did you invite your readers to work with you in a specific offer email?** How many times? You may need to increase the frequency of your offer newsletters.

- **Is your description of your 1:1 offering clear, compelling, and relevant to your readers?** Do you make it obvious who would be a good fit, what changes they could expect after working together, and how to sign up?

- **Double check all links in your offer newsletters and bio** to make sure they are working.

- **If people are clicking the "work with me" button in your offer newsletter but not signing up to work with you, review and revise your website sales page**.

Newsletter Tip: Wasting your time and/or wasting the readers' time

A common fear I hear is that writers don't want their newsletters to be just another piece of junk in someone's already crowded inbox. Also, people don't want to spend time and energy writing a newsletter that no one really wants to read and that won't make a difference.

First, the very fact that you're worried about this tells me that you're unlikely to be selfishly sending out pushy sales messages without providing any other value.

It may take you some time to find a rhythm and to find your voice. Some of your newsletters may be rough around the edges or may not quite hit the mark in terms of voice or vibe or content. And, overall, if you follow the steps listed here and listen carefully for feedback while regularly writing and sending, your newsletter will get better.

If something is useful to you or interesting to you or helpful to you (or an earlier version of yourself), it will likely be the same for others who are reading. Filter your ideas with your reader in mind, and you'll be moving in the right direction.

Remember that **your messages don't need to be life-changing, comprehensive, or authoritative to make a difference.** You can touch people by sharing something real, by being empathetic, by sharing something useful, or by questioning a paradigm. Small is beautiful and helpful, and in many cases, small is more digestible and less overwhelming than bigger, longer content.

You'll know if you're wasting your time because you'll be looking at your results at least every season as described in this chapter. You'll know if you're wasting your readers' time if you start sending messages that you don't care much about and that don't really sound or feel like you. If this happens, it's time to reevaluate your marketing and promotion strategy to decide if you want to make any changes.

Chapter 18
Conclusion

You've made it to the end! I hope you're finishing this book feeling encouraged and even excited about your newsletter. **If you can't implement everything I've recommended right away, don't worry. You don't need to do everything I've recommended to have a newsletter that works.**

The most important things are that your newsletter:

- Sounds and feels like you

- Supports or provides value to your readers

- Is sent regularly

If you can do these things, you'll be well on your way to sending a newsletter that makes a difference to you, your readers, and your business.

Final pieces of advice

Make your newsletter into something that feels creative, fun, and/or meaningful. There isn't a single right way to write or send a newsletter.

Bring yourself into your newsletters. Your stories, ideas, thoughts, perspectives, and experiences matter. Showing who you are gives readers something with which to resonate.

Aim to serve your readers and your community with your writing. Your newsletter may be just what someone needs to hear today.

Make offers periodically so that people know you're available to help them.

Keep writing and sending regularly. Your newsletter won't work if you don't send it. Sometimes your newsletters will be subpar, and other times they'll be extraordinary. You can't always predict which ones will land in which category.

Remember that writing a newsletter is one way of building trust. Trust takes time. Your newsletter won't bring in new clients instantaneously, and that's okay. Writing and sending regularly is a creative practice whose results build on themselves.

Evaluate your progress each season. Don't keep doing the same thing if there aren't at least some small signs it's working. Get outside eyes on your plan if needed.

And finally, believe your intuition. If a topic or resource is interesting to you, it's likely interesting to your readers as well. If something feels off, listen to your inner voice and make a change. You don't need any special powers to write a newsletter. Show up from a place of authenticity, send with the intention to help your community, and trust that your voice matters.

Next steps

All that's left to do is to write your next newsletter. If you're in need of tips and encouragement or even a real-time newsletter writing session, check out the Write Better Newsletters resources page: https://www.writebetterletters.com/resources.

If this book has been helpful, would you take a moment to review it? It makes all the difference.

I'm wishing you all the best and cheering you on.

Happy writing! – Camille

Appendix 1: Newsletter Topic Ideas

If you need some suggestions to get your juices flowing, here are a few:

- Write about one thing you can see on or around your desk. How does this relate to your readers? Why do you have it on your desk? Would it be useful to your readers in any way?

- Tell the story of the time you first got into this field. Keep it very short. What's one interaction or experience that started the ball rolling?

- What is one thing you wish most clients knew before they started to work with you?

- What's one thing that frustrates you about your field?

- Write about a mistake you made when you first started doing this work (or when you started applying it to yourself).

- What does your family think you do?

- A book I've read recently that made a difference... Here's how it's relevant to the work I do/the readers of this newsletter.

- Five of the resources/tools/websites you most often recommend to clients.

- What is one thing that needs to be debunked in your field?

Appendix 2: When You Don't Feel Motivated

Now that you know how much goes into writing a newsletter, I hope you have a deeper appreciation for the top-notch newsletters you receive. There are likely a handful of newsletters you love and enjoy receiving. These are the ones that are super helpful and maybe even feel like they were written specifically for you. **If you receive newsletters like this, I strongly encourage you to reply to the author and let them know that you loved that issue (or that you love their newsletter in general).**

There are a few reasons to do this:

1. **When you're feeling stuck and demotivated, doing something nice for someone else feels good.** It can jostle you out of a funk or at least move you in the right direction. It doesn't matter if the newsletter writer writes back or not; taking a moment to feel grateful for receiving something helpful and to know that you've helped someone else have a better day simply feels good.

2. **Honoring that someone's message made a difference for you helps them know that their work has meaning**. It touched you, and that's important to acknowledge. Even if it's a newsletter with one thousand or ten thousand or one hundred thousand subscribers, the author is still a person. A human person with feelings who's put work into providing a service for their readers. These human touches are important, and they matter.

3. **You would be surprised at how few people do this**. Even exceptionally large newsletters may not have many replies on any given day. If you reply authentically and kindly when a message makes a difference, you may start to build a relationship with the sender.

If you do this, don't expect or anticipate an answer. Don't ask for one. Keep the message short. Explain, in detail if you can, why the message mattered to you. Or share that you passed the message along to your client, friend, mailing list, social media followers, etc. because it [say something nice]. Thank them for the time it takes to send a good newsletter and say you appreciate theirs.

That's it. You'll feel better, you'll make someone's day, and you just may start building a relationship that will grow in unexpected ways.

Appendix 3: CAN-SPAM, GDPR, and Other Regulations

First, please know that I am not a lawyer or an expert in email compliance. I did want to share some of the guidelines and regulations that apply to people who send newsletters for business purposes. These laws and regulations change frequently. **Please verify that you are acting within the bounds of the law by consulting an expert, reviewing the text of any relevant laws and regulations yourself, and investigating which laws and regulations apply in the region or country/countries where you live and work.** If you use a respected ESP, provide clear opt-in forms that ensure people know they are subscribing to your newsletter, have a defined privacy policy, and don't include false or misleading information in your newsletter or subject lines, you'll likely be all set.

CAN-SPAM

The CAN-SPAM Act (which stands for "Controlling the Assault of Non-Solicited Pornography and Marketing Act of 2003") is a federal law that sets rules for commercial email sent to people within the US. **It requires senders to include a clear unsubscribe option, prohibits deceptive subject lines, and mandates that commercial emails include the sender's physical address.** The Federal Trade Commission enforces this law. The important bits are that if you are sending commercial email, your subject and "from" lines need to be truthful and clear, you must include a physical address in all emails (PO boxes are okay), and you need to have a quick and easy way for people to unsubscribe. ESPs help quite a bit to ensure compliance with these regulations.

- You can read the full text of the CAN-SPAM Act here: https://www.ecfr.gov/current/title-16/chapter-I/subchapter-C/part-316.

- And you can read the Federal Trade Commission's Compliance Guide for Businesses here: https://www.ftc.gov/business-guidance/resources/can-spam-act-compliance-guide-business.

GDPR

GDPR stands for the General Data Protection Regulation, which is a comprehensive data protection law in the European Union that went into effect in 2018. This regulation applies to you if you collect data (including email addresses, names, or IP addresses) from people in the EU. **The key points relevant to most newsletter writers are that you must be able to show that you have explicit consent from someone before collecting their data.** This means that they should be consenting specifically to join your newsletter when they sign up. If you offer a freebie, they must consent both to receiving the freebie AND subscribing to your newsletter. Most people recommend having a checkbox for each of these on your sign-up form to avoid confusion.

GDPR also dictates that subscribers must be able to find out how you will use their data, how long you will keep it, etc. They must be able to request access to their data and to find out how it is being used and can request that you delete their data at any time. These things should be covered in your website's privacy policy. **For clarity, it is a good idea to link to your website's privacy policy from your subscribe form.**

- You can read the full legislation: https://gdpr-info.eu/.

- If you don't have a privacy policy on your website, go ahead and create one now. There are many free privacy policy generators online, or you can purchase one as part of a bundle of contract templates from Braden Drake's Contract Club for a one-time fee (https://notavglaw.com/club) . Services like iubenda and Termly will also help you create free privacy policies for your website.

Federal Trade Commission Act

The Federal Trade Commission Act states that:

- Advertising must be truthful and non-deceptive.

- Advertisers must have evidence to back up their claims.

- Advertisements cannot be unfair.

A few ways this may apply to newsletter writers are that **you must clearly disclose any affiliate or referral links you include in a newsletter (or on your website), you cannot make unsupported claims about how effective your services or products are (either directly or indirectly/implied claims), and if you use reviews or testimonials, they must be accurate and not misleading** (e.g., reviews should not be from people who had exceptionally good results if that is not the experience of most of your clients). You must have substantiation if you use reviews or testimonials in your advertising, meaning that if someone says they achieved a specific result, you must be able to show proof that they did achieve that result.

- FTC's Advertising Basics for Small Businesses: https://www.ftc.gov/business-guidance/resources/advertising-fa qs-guide-small-business

- The FTC's Guide for Platforms on Featuring Online Customer Reviews: https://www.ftc.gov/business-guidance/resources/featuring-onl ine-customer-reviews-guide-platforms

State-specific laws

Many states are implementing their own data protection regulations. For example, the California Consumer Privacy Act applies to certain businesses that collect personal information from California residents and requires businesses to inform consumers about what personal data is collected/used, to allow consumers to request access to their data, and to provide consumers a way to opt out of the sale of personal data. By following the guidelines of GDPR and the CAN-SPAM Act, most of us will also be in compliance with these state laws as well, and it is important to stay up to date with the regulations to ensure that you're on the right side of the law as these rules change and new ones are added.

Overview

Don't be deceptive, make sure people know that they are subscribing to a newsletter, give everyone a way to unsubscribe from marketing emails, use an ESP to manage your list, and include a privacy policy on your subscribe forms. If you are offering a freebie, give EU users (and everyone, preferably!) the option to only receive the freebie or to receive the freebie and subscribe to your list.

Appendix 4: Resources

For direct links to these and other resources, please visit the book resources page: https://www.writebetterletters.com/resources.

Write Better Newsletters: The Newsletter

Sign up for Camille's newsletter about newsletters for tips, encouragement, and ideas. The paid version of the newsletter offers the chance to attend monthly newsletter-writing sessions with peer feedback and to watch Camille's video review of a newsletter draft each month. Subscribe at https://www.writebetterletters.com.

Newsletters writers mentioned in *Write Better Newsletters*

- Kristen Mastel

- Mark Silver

- Liane Moccia

- George Kao

- Justin Welsch

- Leonie Dawson

- Bonnie Rose Weaver

- Ann Handley

- Kendra Adachi

- Kendra Payne

- Austin Kleon

- Camille Freeman

Books and resources mentioned in *Write Better Newsletters*

- *Several Short Sentences About Writing* by Verlyn Klinkenborg

- *Struggle Care* podcast with KC Davis

- Upwork for hiring contractors to help with tech tasks

- Pexels and Pixabay for images in the public domain

- Fontjoy for finding fonts that go together

- More information about Creative Commons Licensing

- Camille's Seasonal Planning Workshops

- Focusmate for virtual coworking

- *Heart-Centered Business* by Mark Silver for help explaining what you do

- Jay Acunzo for help telling your stories in a meaningful way

- *Learning How to Learn* online course with Barbara Oakley

- Contract Clubfrom NotAvg Law for contract templates at a very affordable price

- Termly and iubenda to make sure your website is compliant with privacy laws

Access updated links to these and other resources on the *Write Better Newsletters* Resources page: https://www.writebetterletters.com/resources/ .

Acknowledgements

Write Better Newsletters was my 2024 project. I began in January and wrapped up about a year later, following the process laid out in Rob Fitzpatrick's excellent book, *Write Useful Books*. This book was made possible by the Useful Books framework, as well as the merry band of writers from the Useful Authors community who met week after week for writing groups: Brian, Lou, Jason, Marjorie, Enrika, Liz, Linda, Ruby, and Adam, among many others. I would never have written this book without putting my behind in the seat (putting my face in the Zoom square?) along with all of you.

I also extend my gratitude to the many people who signed up for pilot versions of my online newsletter course and who were beta readers for early versions of this book. Each of you provided thoughtful suggestions and encouragement that made the final product into something much better than it would have otherwise been.

I am so very grateful to have the best kinds of friends and colleagues – ones who could easily be competitors but who are instead collaborators, who are kind and supportive and encouraging: Bevin, Megan, Lavonzell, Maria, Erika, and Jiling, just to name a few. I give thanks to my mentors and teachers who helped me believe first that I could write a newsletter worth reading and then that I could write a book worth reading: Illana Burk, George Kao, Mark Silver, Beth Pickens, Rachael Cook, and others.

Many thanks to Tracie Kendziora for help editing and proofreading.

To my family, Mom and Dad, Molly, Robin, Matt, Henry, and June: You're the best.

And, of course, to everyone who has signed up for my newsletters along the way: Thank you. Your encouragement and support – and the fact that you kept reading, clicking, replying, and signing up for things – made this book possible.

About the Author

Camille Freeman has been a practicing herbalist, nutritionist, and educator since 2003. In 2018, she left social media and began marketing her business primarily through a weekly newsletter. Since then, she's mentored hundreds of other practitioners as they grow and build their businesses both with and without social media.

Through her business Bloom and Grow Nutrition, Camille mentors practicing herbalists and nutritionists, and offers continuing education courses for clinicians. She also hosts the podcast *In the Clinic with Camille* (https://www.intheclinic.com).

Camille holds a doctorate in clinical nutrition from MUIH (now part of Notre Dame of Maryland), as well as master's degrees in both herbal medicine from MUIH and physiology from Georgetown University. You can learn more about Camille on her website: https://www.camillefreeman.com.

Thank you for reading + a request

I hope you've found *Write Better Newsletters* to be helpful as you build or revamp your newsletter.

If you enjoyed the book and found value in reading it, would you be so kind as to leave a rating or review? Your feedback will help me improve future editions and makes the book more visible to other practitioners who may be looking for ways to build their own practices.

You can leave a review on:

- Amazon

- Goodreads or Storygraph

- The book's website (www.writebetterletters.com/reviews)

- Wherever you purchased the book

I'm so very grateful for your support.

Warmly,

Camille

www.ingramcontent.com/pod-product-compliance
Lightning Source LLC
LaVergne TN
LVHW051332050326
832903LV00031B/3487